Motion

The Art of
Moving Forward
by Creating Change

Aileen Sideris

Motion: The Art of Moving Forward by Creating Change, by Aileen Sideris.

Published by Aileen Sideris.

PO Box 20145, New York, NY 10014.

Printed in the United States of America.

While the author has made every effort to provide accurate external resources, the author does not assume any liability for changes to these resources after publication.

"I learned this, at least, by my experiment; that if one advances confidently in the direction of his dreams, and endeavors to live the life which he has imagined, he will meet with a success unexpected in common hours."

Henry David Thoreau, Walden

To my partner, best friend,
and love of my life.

To the people who have stood by me
when I needed their support the most.

To those who believed in me and
gave me a shot when no-one else would.

To the challenges I've faced that have
turned me into the person I am today.

The gratitude I have for you all is unwavering and never-ending.

Thank you.

Table of Contents

Introduction

What's *Motion*?

Motion is a methodology and a simple, effective way of attaining your goals. It breaks goal-setting processes into realistic, actionable steps to help you succeed. You are the provider of the results. Your actions that will take you to your goal.

Motion makes the path clear and gives you simple steps that make the seemingly impossible, possible, no matter how big or small your goals are.

By providing clear and understandable life management instructions and combining them with meditations and affirmations that anyone can practice daily, you'll be able to advance at an accelerated pace toward your goals.

It doesn't matter what your position is in life, how much money you have, where you live, or even how big or small your goals are. *Motion* is scalable and can be used by anybody, in any country, of any age to achieve any goal.

Motion in Action

Gaining Clarity. What do you truly want, and what has been standing in your way?

Research, Resources & Risks. Perform research, establish the resources you'll need, and prepare for any potential roadblocks you may encounter on your path to success.

Paving the Way. Overcome obstacles using proven approaches that will make achieving your goals effortless.

Success from Humble Beginnings. Stay motivated on your journey by reading the life stories of individuals who had humble beginnings, yet saw unimaginable success.

Pass it On. By the end of this book, you'll have the knowledge you need to accomplish your goals and an awakened faith in yourself and your capabilities. Now that you know how to succeed, help others do the same.

◆

I used to see the pursuit of my goals as a hill that I had to climb when, in fact, it was more like a staircase. Each attempt would bring me one step closer, sometimes slowly, sometimes more quickly, but always closer.

By stopping on each step and looking back, analyzing what I had learned, I became well-informed on how to climb the stairs more quickly. Placing goals at the top of a staircase instead of a mountain will make it easier to reach the top.

You have to believe success is possible to succeed.

From a young age, I would listen to people when they told me I couldn't do certain things or couldn't live a certain kind of life. Feeling deflated at first, I'd soon gather the courage I needed to push past those judgments and create my own path to success.

I would think, "If other people can do it, then why can't I?" I believe this line of thinking allowed me to make great strides in life.

Motion takes an interlacing approach, combining positive thinking with actionable steps that let you know you're on track to achieving your goals.

Unimaginable Success, Attained

We later explore the lives of some of the world's most talented and successful individuals. So, how did they become so successful?

Although greatness was achieved, for these individuals and many others, it didn't come easily. It took hard work, determination, and an unwavering belief in their own abilities.

Sometimes all we see is the success people have, but it's important to remember where they came from, what opportunities they had and didn't have, and how they made their own luck.

Oprah Winfrey's mother was a housemaid, and her father was a barber. Even with a modest start in life, according to Forbes, her net worth is estimated to be $2.6B.[1]

Stephen King has, "...sold an estimated 350 million books."[2] It's almost inconceivable to think of him as a gas station attendant or to think of his wife as an employee of *Dunkin' Donuts*, yet these job titles are part of their origin stories.

Actress Kate Winslet, who has been in over 50 feature films and has received over 90 awards to date, was working at a local sandwich shop when she got the news that she'd landed her first major role in the movie Heavenly Creatures. It would be this performance that would propel her into stardom after receiving countless rejections.

Barack Obama was a recipient of The Nobel Peace Prize. At one point, he was earning $13k per year at his first job out of college in Chicago. His then-

---

[1] Forbes. "#12 Oprah Winfrey Entrepreneur, Personality, Philanthropist."

[2] Heller. "Meet the writers." The Washington Post.

girlfriend Michelle even recalls the giant hole on the passenger-side floor of the car he was driving when they first started dating.

How did these accomplished people achieve such grand successes despite their modest backgrounds? We explore their early lives and all of the events that, combined, turned them into the people they are today.

The Power of Believing in Yourself

Growing up, I was surrounded by loving parents, family members, friends, schoolteachers, and acquaintances. For the most part, the people in my life had my best interests at heart. They wanted to teach me how the world worked. Their goals were to better prepare me for the hurdles I might face one day.

Unfortunately, their perceptions of how the world worked were often limiting and disappointing. Those words of encouragement that I heard as a child, "You can be anything you want to be when you grow up," faded away as I got older.

Words of encouragement were turned into dejections and appeals *to be more realistic* and to *shoot for more attainable goals*.

I don't believe the people in my life carried any malicious intent. These were just their thoughts, most likely instilled in *them* as they were growing up. They may have been trying to save me time, money and heartache, but that advice only serves in ending dreams and not building them.

Many of the people I grew up with didn't believe *they* were capable of achieving their own goals. That's why they tried to discourage me from reaching my own. That distinction took me *years* to finally realize, but once I did, it changed my perspective forever.

Many friends and family members seemed to believe that dreams should be left for the dreamers, and unlike dreamers, they were realists. Ironically, we would have been on the same page if their reality were a more hopeful one.

But instead, their realities were stifling and only included possibilities they saw being achieved by people around them. As a result, anything outside of the norm became *unrealistic*.

Many people told me I couldn't achieve my dreams for one seemingly legitimate reason or another. So, is it a coincidence that these same people hadn't reached their own dreams?

I don't think it's a coincidence. I believe there's a direct correlation between your mindset, what you believe to be possible, and what becomes your reality. If you don't allow yourself to consider that something is in the realm of possibility, then how can *any* action take place?

Your dreams can either live or cease to exist, depending on whether you believe they're within your reach.

It's risky asking the people around you if they think it's possible to reach specific goals if those same people have yet to reach their own. But, until they have, or someone close to them has, you might hear the same "words of wisdom" that I heard: "You have to be lucky... You need to be born rich...You need natural talent...Talent can't be learned...You won't have the time...It's like winning the lotto..."

Lies, lies, and more lies. Well-intended lies but lies, nonetheless. Maybe this advice *can* help bring you closer to your goals, but only if you use it to fuel the fire that burns inside you. That's really the only thing you should do with advice like this: burn it.

Without belief, there would be no concept of what that ideal life would look like, and if you don't believe you can have something, how can you carry out actions to achieve that thing?

Without thoughts, there are no actions.
Without actions, change is impossible.

What Does Success Mean to You?

To one person, success may mean finishing college, finding a good job, getting married, and having children. If that's what success means to you, great! But, we're all individuals, meaning "success" changes from person to person.

Essentially, you'll have to define success based on what success means to you and you alone. And if you do that, you'll stop letting others define it for you.

Become comfortable with the fact that you'll never be what every single person wants you to be. If you want to be happy, you'll have to accept yourself as a whole, even if key figures in your life don't. The happiest version of yourself will be the one that's been fully realized. The true you.

If you can let go of who other people *think* you should be, then you'll be able to reach your fullest potential. Why not start today?

There will be people in your life who are close to you and will look at you curiously, to say the least. They might not understand or approve of your life choices, and they might even see you as a failure. You need to be okay with both.

You have one life to live, and you're living it here and now. Do you want to spend your one precious life simply trying to gain the approval of others?

I have some sobering news. One reason these people may see you as a failure, even when you see yourself as a success, is because they may feel like failures within themselves. That feeling of defeat could be preventing them from being happy for you, and instead, judgments are made based on how you make them feel about themselves.

If they were comfortable with who they were and how they've spent their lives, then their only concern would be your health and happiness. That's it.
They wouldn't put pressure on you to be someone you're not or to live a life you don't want to live.

Another reason could be because they're living in fear. Fear that you'll end up chasing a pipe dream and end up with nothing to show for it.

Whatever their reasons might be, you need to be on the lookout, ready to recognize fear disguised as helpful advice.

We all want the people we care about to be happy and healthy. So, if you're both of those things, shouldn't your loved ones be happy for you, for achieving success as you've defined it? I believe they should be, and I hope they are.

Are you willing to live your life as a different person, spending your time in ways that don't make you feel happy, just because you were trying to make judgmental people *proud of you*? I can think of few things more unreasonable than this. The ironic part?

> *You've let yourself down in your pursuit*
> *of pleasing people who judge you.*

Maybe you have dreams, goals, and aspirations that fall out of social norms. Perhaps you want to be an author, a painter, a performance artist, an actor, or an actress. Maybe you want to start your own business or travel the world and won't be satisfied until you have a stamp in your passport from every single country on the planet!

Don't kid yourself. You might think, "Maybe if I finish my degree...Maybe if I give up music and show them, I'm serious...Maybe if I settle down and get a good job...Maybe *then* they'll respect me. Maybe *then* they'll look at me and see success!"

Wrong! These people don't care about your success. Instead, they care about how you make them feel about themselves.

Turn the tables. Instead of trying to be someone else, inspire others to become the people they've always wanted to be.

Turning Ideas into Realities

If there's a goal you're pursuing that's never been achieved before, then *you* can be the first person to achieve it. Is that hard to believe?

Well, think about this, if people throughout history didn't even *try* to invent something new or come up with a new idea because they didn't think they could, what would the world look like today? Which medicines would be available to us? What kinds of thoughts would we believe about the earth and the universe around us?

We're truly standing on the shoulders of giants. It's because of the individuals who have thought outside of the box and simply tried that we have progressed as much as we have as a people. Allow yourself to discover what you're really capable of accomplishing by simply trying.
Everything that was ever invented or achieved was merely an idea before it became a reality.

Before we do *anything*, we think about doing it and believe it's possible to achieve. This goes for every single action we take. If you didn't think something was possible to do, you wouldn't even try. Knowing that a goal is possible to achieve is always the first step towards reaching it.

◆

Try this thought experiment: think of a goal, any goal. Now, assume that goal is nearly impossible to achieve. You don't know anyone who has personally achieved this goal, so you believe achieving it is reserved for the lucky few.

What does the next step that you take look like on your path towards achieving that goal? Remember, you feel like it's almost impossible to achieve. Your actions will be muted. They'll be toned down. You won't try as hard because, why should you? It's probably not going to happen anyway, right?

Now think of that same goal, but attach a higher probability towards achieving it. Let's pretend like you've heard of a few people attaining this goal. Maybe not your closest friends, but friends of friends. The goal feels way more possible to achieve. Now, what does your next step look like?

It's not a mystery. It's not a blind belief. It's common sense. Your thoughts create your actions. More dreams are born and killed in the mind than by actually trying to achieve them. Choose your thoughts wisely!

This one shift in your line of thinking can literally rearrange every other aspect of your life, bringing you closer to your goals than ever before. It may even allow you to have goals you never thought possible to achieve.

When you truly love who you are, what you do, and how you spend your time, you become an inspiration to others who may feel hopeless in their own situation.

You have the power to change lives by changing your own.

What's "Safe" and "Secure" Anyway?

Some people might tell you that getting and keeping a job until you retire is the safest and most secure route you can take.

If you love what you're doing for a living and look forward to doing it, then your job isn't a job, it's a dream. It's something that satiates you, that you take pride in. However, if you don't feel that way and are only working a job for the "safety and security" you've been taught it provides, then I recommend re-evaluating this approach.

Sometimes it's hard to tell why we're working at a particular job or in a specific career, if not just for the paycheck. So, we make excuses, talk about the friends we have at work, or how we like the schedule. Now, that all may be true, but there's one sure-fire way to find out if you're really in love with your job or if you're just trying to make the best of it.

Ask yourself, would you be working at this job if you were a billionaire? If you had all the money in the world and could do anything with your time, how would you be spending it? If the answer is no, you would not be working at this job every day if you were a billionaire, then perhaps the "safe" and "secure" road isn't for you, and that's ok!

If you do love your job and would do it even if you had all the money in the world, then bravo! I'm thrilled that you found something that you're excited to do every day!

◆

In this context, "safe" and "secure" are often defined as having job security, a steady source of income, and the knowledge that tomorrow will be similar to today. You'll know how much each paycheck will be, and you'll receive annual raises that might exceed the rate of inflation (if you're lucky).

Your job might give you two weeks off each year. But, if you're like so many other Americans, you probably won't even use this small amount of vacation time.

According to an eye-opening article published by The Washington Post in 2019, "...55 percent of

Americans did not use all of their paid vacation time,"[3] referring to the previous year, 2018.

What's ironic about this "secure" route is that it's really anything but. This life path is built on a few assumptions. It assumes that you will live to be in your 60s, and if you do, you will receive retirement benefits and will be able to live off those benefits for the rest of your life.
It assumes that you'll always have enough money to pay for healthcare costs and that your job will always be there. Let's take a closer look at how these assumptions hold up in 2022.

The first assumption is that you will live to see your 60s. You probably will, but there's no guarantee, and who knows what your life will look like by then. You may need to take care of a loved one, or you yourself may be too sick to actually enjoy your hard-earned retirement.

These are harsh realities that you need to face. If this is already hitting too close to home, then you definitely need to make a change. Remember, it's never too late!
I'm not saying you shouldn't plan for the future, because you absolutely should, but what I *am* saying is that you shouldn't wait to start enjoying your life. There's a middle ground, and you can achieve it in the here and now.

---

[3] Sampson. "What does America have against vacation?" The Washington Post.

Another assumption is that you'll be able to live solely on social security and retirement benefits. But, unfortunately, many individuals and families *can't* live on these benefits alone. According to AARP (American Association of Retired Persons), "As of February 2019, more than 20 percent of adults over age 65 are either working or looking for work..."[4] If 1 in 5 (20%) people over the age of 65 still need to work, then what's the point of spending your life working for a company if you still might not be able to support yourself by the end of your career?

You've spent the majority of your life working, you've taken the "safe and secure" route—you should be able to afford healthcare, right? Nope!

According to a survey from West Health and Gallup, "An estimated 7.5 million seniors are unable to pay for medicine prescribed to them because they don't have enough money. And to make the matter worse, seniors reported that 80% of the prescriptions they cannot afford are for a somewhat or very serious health condition."[5]

The last risky assumption you'll make when going down the "safe and secure" route is that your job will always be there, and you'll always have a steady paycheck. Below is an excerpt from an article published by FreshBooks

---

[4] Edleson "More Americans Working or Looking for Work After 65." AARP.

[5] Stevens and Mallory. "US Seniors Pay Billions, yet Many Cannot Afford Healthcare." Gallup News.

titled, "What Percentage of Businesses Fail in the First Year?"

"The small business failure rate will likely remain around 20 percent in 2020. This is the failure rate for businesses that are a year old. The failure rate will be about 30 percent in their second year, 50 percent in their fifth year and 70 percent in their tenth year."[6]

This means that, out of 10 employees who stay at a company that's been in business for 10 or more years, seven of them will need to find a new job. This is because businesses that are in their 10th year have a 70% failure rate. So much for job security.

If the "safe and secure" path is anything but, then why not live the life that will bring you the most happiness, today?

You can spend your whole life waking up early, feeling tired and unfulfilled, just to reach the light at the end of the tunnel—retirement. Once you get there, you may find out that you actually can't afford to stop working. What a terrible outcome after a lifetime of hard work! This is unacceptable, but avoidable.

Some people take the aforementioned route out of fear of doing the things that they really want to do. Others may take this route after experiencing pressure from society, family members, or friends, or because they

---

[6] "What Percentage of Businesses Fail in the First Year? FreshBooks.

don't believe that any other path is possible. Why would we believe that we could break out of this cycle if no one we personally know has, right? This is why we believe the lies: because those lies are all so many of us have ever known or have been surrounded by.

You want a better life with every ounce of your being. So, how can it be yours? How can you wake up every single morning and decide how *you* will spend the day, and who *you* will spend your time with? Will you ever be able to put out that album, sell your own art, start your own company or travel the world? Will you ever be happy, and can you do the "impossible" by breaking the cycle of suffering and freeing yourself from a life of drudgery?

I'm here to tell you that you *can* live your dreams, but only by changing your thoughts and your actions. Start by believing you can. Then, clearly define your goal in order to achieve it.

✧

Gaining Clarity

Gaining Clarity is the first step in the process. Without gaining clarity on your goals, you won't be able to establish time frames around them or know which resources you'll need to achieve success.

If you don't take this as a first step, you're pretty much just going for a drive without a destination, which will most likely land you right back where you started. Clarity provides the foundation that all other steps are built on.

For example, if your goal is to lose weight, but it's not clearly defined, you might tell yourself, "My goal is to lose as much weight as I can, as quickly as possible."

With this as your goal, you may end up *gaining* weight on your "diet" instead of shedding a single pound! That's because goals like these don't have time frames, benchmarks, or mini goals to measure success by.

If you don't have a set number of pounds you'd like to lose, how can you know what your diet should look like or how much exercise you should be getting every day in order to produce the desired results?

If you haven't established a time frame, how do you know the amount of weight you'll need to lose each week in order to hit your mark? You won't know if you're closer or further away from any goal without clearly defining what success means to you and what the reality of that success will look like.

By clearly defining your goal, you're then able to set benchmarks to measure success. These benchmarks are mini-achievements that should be celebrated and acknowledged. There's a path to every goal; this is the first step towards your destination.

Drill Down to What You Really Want

When it comes to goal-setting, you'll want the goals you set for yourself to be as specific as they will be once they're actualized.

You don't just want any car. That's not specific enough. *You want a red 1971 Ford Mustang Mach 1 with a black stripe down the middle.*

You don't want just any house. That's too vague. *You want a one-story, four-bedroom house on an acre of land surrounded by trees and nature.*

You don't want to travel just anywhere. *You want to travel across Europe, starting in Italy and staying there for two months before visiting France for a week, England for two weeks, Ireland and Scotland for another two weeks, and then ending the trip by spending one month in Switzerland.*

You're going to be building your life around your goals, and not the other way around. That's a remarkable difference and one that will empower you and those around you.

Create a clear vision of what your goal
will look like once it's been attained.

If you're still having difficulty specifying your goals, try this: close your eyes and see yourself waking up in your ideal life. Now drill in further.

✧ *I encourage you to answer all questions in the book as you encounter them before moving forward.*

- What do you look like/What does life feel like as soon as you wake up in the morning?

- What kinds of clothes are you pulling out of your closet as you get dressed?

- What does the room you're waking up in feel like?

- Can you smell the fresh pot of coffee brewing from the kitchen?

- Are you about to eat breakfast? What are you going to have?

- How will your day-to-day life improve now that this goal has been completed?

- Will you have more time?

- If so, what will you do with all that extra time?

- Will you learn a new skill, language, or instrument or are you excited to work at the business you founded?

- What kind of business have you started and what do you do there?

- What does a day in your new role look like?

- Are you in an office and if you are, is it modern and trendy, or is it classic and traditional? Maybe the business is remote, and your morning commute consists of passing the living room and petting the dog before sitting at your chair in your home office.

- How does it feel to sit in your home office and start your day?

- If you end up having more money from achieving your goals, how will you spend it?

- Are there any places you've always wanted to visit or things you've always wanted to do?

These thoughts are fundamental to have as early on in your journey as possible. For you to live this life, you have to see it first. Nothing is more true than this.

When you're hungry, you think about what you want to eat before you even get up and start preparing a meal. You think about when you'll be eating, how good the food will taste, and how satisfied you'll feel when you're finished. You *know* you can have that meal, so you plan it out and fully expect to have it soon.

Now that you've given it some thought and know what you want, you go to your kitchen and cook up your favorite meal. Because you knew it was possible, you entertained the thought and followed it through to completion.

We can take that same approach for our goals and dreams. We have believed naysayers' lies about what's *possible* and *realistic,* and their lies became our truths. Those truths destroyed our dreams before we could ever have them. Now, it's time to get back on track!

Why Do You Want to Achieve This Goal?

Your reasons for wanting to achieve a certain goal are as important as the goal itself. If it's to please a spouse, co-worker, family member or friend, I highly suggest you take a pause here to reevaluate. Start to focus your attention inward. It's not the easiest thing to do, but it must be done. You owe it to yourself.

The only reason you should be in pursuit of any goal in life
is because the act of accomplishing that goal
will fulfill you like nothing else can.

You cannot and should not live for anyone else's
approval, no matter how much you love or admire them.

If you're seeking approval from other people around you, you will have to stop that right here and now

The only person whose approval
you should seek is your own.

It doesn't matter if the whole world sees you as a success or a failure. How do *you* see yourself? What do *you* define as success? What do *you* truly want in life? It's not what will make others happy or proud. It's what will make you happy and proud of yourself.

You may not receive support from anyone else around you. Sadly, that is a possibility. I do wish that you and everyone else in the world did receive support and encouragement to follow dreams and pursue goals, but that support isn't always available. While it's very nice to have, luckily, it's not necessary to be successful. What is required is unwavering faith in yourself and your own abilities.

*You have to be your own biggest supporter,
your own ardent advocate.*

*You have to be a defender of dreams, goals, and big
ideas that others mistakenly call impossible.*

You'll need to have a strong demeanor, one that doesn't flinch when told, "You will never succeed!" Now, you can laugh at declarations like these. The same way you'd laugh if someone told you the sun won't be rising tomorrow morning. Laugh because you know it's not true.

You will show the people around you just how dedicated you are to achieving your goals, and in doing so, they'll be inspired to create similar positive changes in their own lives.

How Will You Feel Once This Goal Has Been Accomplished?

o Will you feel relieved or excited after your mission has been accomplished?

o Will you take some satisfaction in knowing that you've proved the cynics wrong?

o   How proud will you be knowing that you've become an inspiration to others?

o   Does a wave of calm rush over you when thinking about how you'll feel once this goal has been completed?
     Maybe, you've never felt this level of ease before. Maybe you have, but only in small doses.

o   Will you feel free of the stress, anxiety, and doubt you've been carrying?

o   Will you feel excited to start your day now that every day feels as relaxed as a Saturday?

o   Will you feel surprised, maybe even shocked, at the fact that you were able to achieve this level of success?

The reality of what you'll feel after your goal has been completed is thrilling in itself. For many people, their dreams have been with them for years. To see their dreams fully realized is a dream in and of itself.
     Accomplishing your goals can have powerful, lasting effects on your personal outlook, daily mood and energy levels. The mere act of accomplishment will show you that you *can* achieve success and that dreams can

be turned into realities. Having that knowledge will make future goals easier to attain, and success goes on and on.

◆

After visualizing your goals and what living your dream life feels like, you may find that you aren't as sure as you once were that this is the right goal for you to attain. Maybe you're just not as enthusiastic about it, or maybe you've discovered a new passion that you're much more excited to pursue.

It's perfectly alright if that happens. It's best to come to those conclusions as quickly as possible, allowing you to divert from the current path and create a new one.
Analyze what attracted you to your original dream life in the first place and also the things that made you unsure if it would be right for you. It's a good practice to go through these steps and to realign your goals as often as needed.

Life is constantly in flux, and moving from one objective to another may just be part of your process until you zero in on the goal that you really want to achieve. Allow yourself this flexibility.

Conquering Limiting Beliefs

Start off by asking yourself, what has really stopped me from pursuing and/or reaching my goal in the past? This will be one of the most challenging questions you'll need to answer, but be sure to answer it as thoughtfully and honestly as possible.

Only you need to know the answer to this question, but knowing it will allow you to push past those old roadblocks and move into your new life.

For some, a lack of resources such as time and money could be reasons why success hasn't been achieved yet. For others, it could be circumstances beyond their control, like needing to care for a loved one or facing illness themselves.

Some factors could have made reaching your goals more challenging, but there's always a workaround and some way of being happy and feeling successful. Instead of casting blame on yourself or other factors, try to find ways to reach your goals, despite any roadblocks that may be in the way.

If you have commitments and responsibilities to loved ones, for example, I believe there are ways that can allow you to fulfill those commitments, while also pursuing your dream. It's essential that you figure out how to incorporate your goals into your daily life, even if it's only on a small scale to start.

Think and focus on potential solutions and scenarios that will allow you to have it all and work backward from there. Explore the corridors of your mind that you never realized existed. Find those alternative paths, and don't stop until you do. It's very easy to say, "My life looks this way because of him / her / this moment / this event / these circumstances."

Your life may very well have been permanently altered in a negative way because of an event or a person, and if that's the case, you might have extra work ahead of you, but that doesn't mean you can't still live your ideal life.

I don't deny that things happen. Sometimes they're good, and sometimes they're very challenging, or just plain awful, but we have to push forward, and we can't allow outside forces to define us or set boundaries on what we're able to achieve.

Living with these events defining us will only prevent future success and happiness from entering our lives. Learn from these events as much as you can and move on from them.

Moving on doesn't happen in a day. It happens in a million small moments, and it's the culmination of those moments that allow us to heal.

Start telling a different story.
You have the power to change the narrative, today.

Below are potential roadblocks you may have been faced with while pursuing your goals in the past:

My partner didn't want me to, so I never tried.

My family thought I was crazy and making a mistake. They fought with me at the thought of me following my passion, so I gave it up to make them happy.

I could never take the kids with me while traveling. Do you know how hard it is to travel with children? Maybe when I retire, and the kids are older, perhaps then I can travel...

I can't leave school. I'd be letting my parents down. I gave up my dream of playing music to make my parents proud.

Those are just a few of the countless roadblocks that may have completely halted the pursuit of passions, dreams, and goals in life.

We can take control of our lives and we don't need anyone's approval to do so.

When you allow others to dictate how you will live, you're giving them your power. The good news is that even the act of giving your power away is something within your control. It was always yours to give and yours to take back.

Motion is about taking charge of your life.
You are the decision-maker.
You are the game-changer.

One of the problems is that we've been conditioned to believe that we don't actually control our lives.

Following are some more lies we've been taught:

Our lives control us, and we have
little say in the matter.

Your lot in life is predetermined before you're born, and you can't ever escape it, no matter how hard you try.

You will always be right where you are, and you're powerless to make a change. People never change.

You're incapable of changing your circumstances, such as the job you work at, where you live, and how you spend your time.

You won't ever live your dreams. Dreams are for other people to live, and you're just not one of the lucky few.

Yup. Powerless. As you were reading the above, did you feel like it was a little, ridiculous? It seems ludicrous to say that you can't leave your job or change where you live, but the truth is that many people feel this way and believe it to be true, which keeps them in bad situations. So many people live where they live, work where they work, and, well, that's that. They've relinquished all their power and have thrown down their swords. They stopped fighting for what they wanted because they didn't believe any other options were available to them.

There's only one decision-maker, decider and ruling body over your life, and that's you.

This is a reality that's as empowering as it is frightening because now you're forced to re-evaluate your own life, but that's a good thing. Re-evaluate away! This is the time to feel strong and empowered because you are. You're examining your past decisions, which is part of the process of taking control of your choices and the paths you follow.

Evaluate Previous Successes & Missteps

If you've tried to accomplish your goals in the past but feel like you've been unsuccessful in your attempts, don't worry! You're actually ahead of the pack, and I'll explain how.

You've not just been staring at the pool waiting to jump in, you *have* jumped in, and that experience alone is priceless. You've made actionable attempts, and your learnings from those attempts can be used as stepping stones toward your success.

By examining what you've already tried in the past, you'll be able to make informed decisions on how to proceed in the future. When evaluating what you've done previously, you'll want to decide:

o   Whether or not you should make those same attempts again.
o   If you are going to make those same attempts, should you alter them in any way, in order to see better results?
o   Perhaps, you shouldn't make those same moves again, since they've proven to be fruitless. If that's the case, what will you try instead?

You may feel like you've been spinning your wheels, working hard to achieve your goals, only to see minuscule advancements that are producing few results. In situations like these, look at historical results from all of your attempts.

Which attempts have you seen the greatest benefits from, and which ones have brought you the smallest gains?

You'll have more time and energy by pursuing the actions that are yielding the highest rewards and discontinuing or altering other attempts that have been less effective.

Shifting gears can be challenging, especially if you've spent a long period of time focusing on one initiative. This might be an initiative that you had hoped would lead you to your destination. Maybe it still will, but is there any evidence to back that up, or is there perhaps another way you'll be able to achieve greater results?

The wait/walk dilemma is one we've all faced at one point in our lives or another. It's when you've been waiting for a bus for a long time, and now have to decide whether you should keep waiting since you've already been there so long, or if you should just walk, instead? You've already put in so much time waiting for the bus, you may as well keep waiting, right?

Not in my opinion. At some point, you have to ask yourself if it's worth it to keep waiting for a bus that may never come. I want to get to my destination as quickly as possible, and if that bus isn't coming, I will find another way. Allow yourself the flexibility to change course. Getting to your destination may be easier than you think once you decide to stop waiting.

Motivating Factors

You'll also want to establish your motivating factors for attaining this goal. By digging deeper, you're increasing your determination while exploring parts of yourself you may not have known were there.

By exploring your true motivating factors for pursuing a goal, you may find out that you want to accomplish something for the wrong reasons.

Maybe you have a goal you'd like to accomplish in the hopes that, through your success, you'll gain validation or respect from society, family, friends, or peers. If that's your primary motivating factor, then you'll have to reassess what's truly important to you. You can continue pursuing the same goal, but reframe the goal so that you're achieving it for yourself instead.

When framing goals, be sure to keep them positive. If you do have a weight loss goal, instead of thinking:
"I hate my body and want to lose weight, so others will like me more," you can create a healthier goal. Such as:
"I love my body so much that I want to treat it better and make sure it's running at peak performance. I already feel beautiful, but I want to lose weight for myself so that I can improve my health and well-being. I can achieve this through a healthy diet and by exercising regularly."

Your full goal may look something like this:
"I will be losing 20 pounds in order to improve my health. I will lose the weight safely, and I'm alright with it taking up to eight weeks, as long as the weight stays off. In that time, I'm going to establish healthy, long-lasting, positive lifestyle habits. Those habits will include exercising at least 150 minutes per week, practicing intermittent fasting, and reducing my intake of refined sugar, fried, and processed foods. This will ensure I'm always feeling healthy and energized."

This is a goal that can be analyzed and measured. It gives you clear benchmarks to hit, reasons for achieving the goal, and a long-term action plan on how you're going to turn it into a reality. You won't just be on a diet with this goal. Diets are often followed and then forgotten. Instead, you'll be embarking on a lifestyle upgrade that will leave you feeling healthier and happier.

Documenting your journey could help you stay motivated and keep you on track. Log the steps you're taking to reach your goals as well as any missteps you may have experienced along the way. These aren't failures but are instead part of the natural process of goal achievement.

When you lack motivation, reread older entries to give yourself a jolt of energy. It'll help you remember all the great progress you've already made and why you started this journey in the first place.

Establishing Time Frames

You're going to want to define a time frame for achieving your goal. We'd all like to achieve our goals as quickly as possible, but depending on your goal, certain steps will need to be taken to accomplish it. You'll need to figure out your ideal time frame for reaching this goal, based on what you think you might need to do to achieve it.

For example, if your goal is to learn Italian, then completing this goal will depend on how often you're using the language and how much exposure to the language you have. But remember, you'll first have to define what "completing the goal" means. Is it defined as the number of phrases and words you know, or is it based on how easy it becomes to understand a certain Italian movie?

Clearly define success to succeed.

For example, if your goal is to become a doctor, there's no rushing it. You will need to go through all of the required schooling and studies in order to accomplish your goal, but you know that once you do, you will be a licensed doctor.

A goal like this one can't be accomplished fully in one day, but you *can* accomplish mini goals related to it on a daily, weekly, and monthly basis.

Based on your goal, what is a reasonable amount of time that you can accomplish it in? Now that you know how long it can take to accomplish your goal, you'll want to establish two time frames: the earliest time frame you'd like to complete your goal and the latest.

Setting up your earliest and latest goal completion times will help to do two things: first, you'll have an ideal target to hit, which will expedite the time it takes to complete the goal. Second, by establishing the latest time that the goal can be completed by, you're giving yourself a hard deadline.

If you think, "One day I'll learn Italian," I can say with a great deal of certainty that you may never learn to speak Italian. By establishing realistic time frames, you're drawing a line in the sand that you're not allowing yourself to cross.

Remember, necessity is the mother of invention.
If you create a need to succeed, you will.

Creating Milestones

On your path to accomplishing this goal, substeps, or *milestones*, will be set. These will strengthen your resolve and increase your ability to persevere until your goal has been fully realized.

If, as part of your weight loss goal, you set a milestone for yourself of losing five pounds in two weeks, then when you lose those five pounds in that time frame, you'll know you're on track to reaching your goal weight.

By the time you reach your goal weight in eight weeks, you'll know how to lose weight and how to keep it off. You would have been living it every single day since you started this journey, and now it'll be easy to maintain.

Your friends and family will eventually redefine how they see you as you have redefined how you see yourself. They will accept that you eat certain foods or stop eating at a certain time of day. They will see your resolve and determination, and they may be inspired to enhance their own lives, too.

Start Living a Version of Your Ideal Life, Today

If your goal is to have a new home, what does it look like? You might be picturing a pristine home with thoughtfully placed furniture and art lining the walls. That life might feel unattainable but look around you. What can you do today that will make you happy when you walk through the door?

Is there any art that you own and just haven't hung up yet? Will moving some furniture around open up the space you're in and make you happier when you come home every day? No, you don't have the dream home yet, but when you do, how will you maintain it? How will it feel to live in it? Start prepping today for your future life.

Take it a step further. Start shopping online for furniture and art for your new home. You don't have to buy the items, yet. Add items to a wishlist that will save them for when you are ready to make a purchase. You may even find that the furniture and art you're looking to buy aren't nearly as unaffordable as you once thought.

You might not be taking your dream European vacation tomorrow, but you know you will be, so start prepping for it, today. Start researching the places that you'll want to visit and the hotels you'll be staying in. Learn more about the customs that are specific to certain areas and start practicing.

Reserve a table at an authentic Italian, Greek or Indian restaurant. Wherever you plan on going, try to start getting a feel for it now. Listen to music, watch movies, and read books from the place you'll be visiting. It's only a matter of time before you take that trip but it's never too early to start feeling happier.

End of Chapter Exercises

Answer the following questions honestly, and to the best of your ability.

- o What is your goal?
  E.g. I want to lose 20 pounds.

  _____

  _____

  _____

- o Why do you want to achieve this goal?
  E.g. I love my body so much that I want to treat it better and make sure it's running at peak performance. I already feel beautiful, but I want to lose weight for myself so that I can improve my health and well-being.

  _____

  _____

o How will you feel once this goal has been achieved, what will your life look like?
E.g. I'll be able to fit into clothes that I haven't worn in years. I'll have enough energy to play with my kids without getting winded. I will feel healthy, energized, and proud of myself for accomplishing my goal.

o What are the things you feel have held you back from achieving this goal, and how will you combat them in the future?
E.g. I've kept food in the house that I know isn't the healthiest for me. I've always been a late-night eater, which I still am, but now having healthier food in the house to snack on will help me stay on track.

_____

_____

_____

o Previously, what attempts have you made to reach
   your goal?
   *E.g. I've tried every fad diet you can think of, but
   I've always lost weight and then put it right back
   on.*

_____

_____

_____

o What went well in each previous attempt at
   completing this goal and what didn't go well? How
   are things going to be different this time?
   *E.g. In some of my previous attempts, I was able
   to lose weight, but not safely and not in a way that*

kept the weight off. Rather than dieting and failing,
I'm permanently changing my habits.

What went well:

_____

_____

_____

What didn't go well:

_____

_____

_____

How are things are going to be different this time:

_____

_____

_____

o   How will you stay motivated, even if things don't
    seem like they're going well?
    *E.g. I've started documenting my journey, and
    when I feel down or fall behind I plan on re-
    reading previous entries to remind myself that my
    goal is possible and I am well on my way to
    achieving it.*

_____

_____

_____

o   In what time frame would you like to accomplish
    this goal?

E.g. I want to lose the weight safely, and I'm alright with it taking up to eight weeks, as long as the weight stays off.

_____

_____

_____

o   What benchmarks or milestones will you be using in order to track success?
E.g. By losing 2.5 pounds per week, I'll know I'm on track to losing 20 pounds in eight weeks.

_____

_____

_____

- What can you do today that will allow you to live a version of your ideal life?
  E. g. I'm going to unpack all of my smaller-sized clothes. I'll also start a collection of clothes that I plan on donating to a charity that will contain larger-sized clothes that won't fit me anymore
- *after I've lost the weight. I'd like to buy some new clothes to celebrate, so I'll start a wishlist on my favorite clothing website, filling it with clothes that are the size I'll be after I reach my weight loss goal.*

_____

_____

_____

Research, Resources & Risks

After you've clearly defined your goal, what steps do you need to take in order to achieve it? Now's the time to establish all the resources you'll need and which of these you already have. What are some of the risks you may encounter while pursuing this goal, and how can you mitigate those risks in order to increase your chances of succeeding?

In this section, you'll design an actionable plan to help you reach your goal. By conducting research at this stage, you'll be building each step of the staircase that will take you to your destination. This way, you'll always know what you need to do and how close to your objective you really are.

Sometimes it may seem like we've set ourselves a goal that is nearly impossible to reach. We may feel like we don't have the time, money, or know-how that's needed, in order to accomplish it. Upon further examination, that goal might not be nearly as difficult to achieve as we once thought, and we may already have many of the resources needed.

By conclusively examining which resources you'll need for each step on your *Path to Success*, you'll be able to plan accordingly.

Risks are inevitable, but that doesn't mean there aren't ways you can prepare for them, and, quite possibly, eliminate some of them altogether. Risk mitigation is crucial and will only help ensure your success while also making your journey as smooth as possible.

Below are a series of steps that, when carried out, will give you a bird's eye view of your goal and what the journey towards it will look like. After that, we'll get into the detail, making the path to success clearer than it ever has been before.

✧ *All tools, websites, and resources mentioned can be found in the end of chapter summaries.*

Research

Identify Each Step You'll Need to Take in Order to Achieve Your Goal

This is the time to plan out what the journey of actually achieving your goal looks like. Abandon false thoughts that make you think, "It's just too expensive. You have to be rich, lucky, or both." Those lies aren't welcome here.

What will it *really* take to achieve success? You might come to find that you're closer to your goal than you thought.

◆

Let's say your goal is to own your dream car. You clearly defined your goal in the previous chapter and know exactly what kind of car you want. Now, you need to find out what you need to do in order to obtain it.

Start by going to Google.com or another search engine of your choice, and perform a search, "buy 1971 Ford Mustang Mach 1 [in your location]." What did you find? Are there any car dealers in your city or state selling your dream car? If there are, how much are they selling it for?

By performing a quick online search, you just learned that the dream car you always thought would be financially out of reach, is actually for sale starting at $15k.

You might need to do some work on the car, or it might be in great shape. Do your due diligence and weigh your options, but at the end of the day, if your dream car costs as much as a car that you're indifferent about purchasing, one that doesn't have half the pizzazz of a 1971 Mustang, then why not get the Mustang?

Now, carry on with your research. What does the journey to buying the car actually look like? Will you need to drive far in order to pick the car up? If you will, how far would you need to travel? There's also insurance, taxes, and making sure your driver's license is valid. You may also want to compile a list of questions to ask the seller of the car before purchasing.

You're defining the very real steps that you'll need to take before buying your dream car. This is one example, but it can be applied to any goal. It's also worth noting that many people don't even get this far. They wrongly assume that their goals are *too big* or *too far out of reach,* and they don't even make it to the research stage! Just by making it this far, you're traveling far ahead of the pack. Break your goal down into steps. Take the smallest step first, and the rest will soon follow.

Creating a *Path to Success*

The *Path to Success* is a clear-cut, well-defined blueprint that includes all the steps needed to achieve your goal. The diagram reads from left to right. The items in the top row are all of the steps needed to accomplish the goal. The items under each step are substeps.

These substeps will be the smaller tasks that are involved in completing each larger step. Some steps will have multiple substeps, such as *Step 1. Research*, which contains three substeps, *A, B,* and *C.* Visualizing all of the elements that make up one major step, will make it easier to complete actions as you move closer and closer to your goal.

You can create the tools in this section on a piece of paper, or by using a spreadsheet or mind-mapping software.
One free mind-mapping tool I've enjoyed using is Miro.com. But, you don't need to use any software. A pen and paper will do just fine.

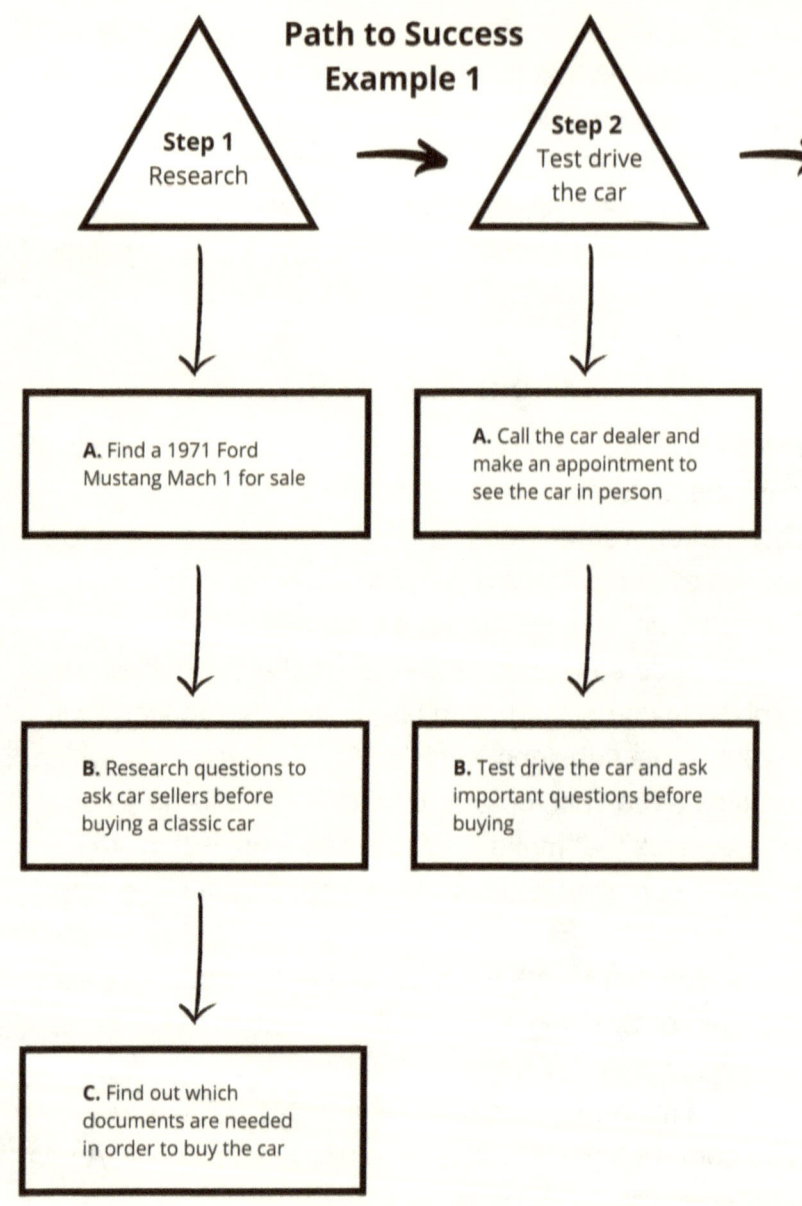

Path to Success
Example 1

Step 1
Research

Step 2
Test drive
the car

A. Find a 1971 Ford
Mustang Mach 1 for sale

A. Call the car dealer and
make an appointment to
see the car in person

B. Research questions to
ask car sellers before
buying a classic car

B. Test drive the car and ask
important questions before
buying

C. Find out which
documents are needed
in order to buy the car

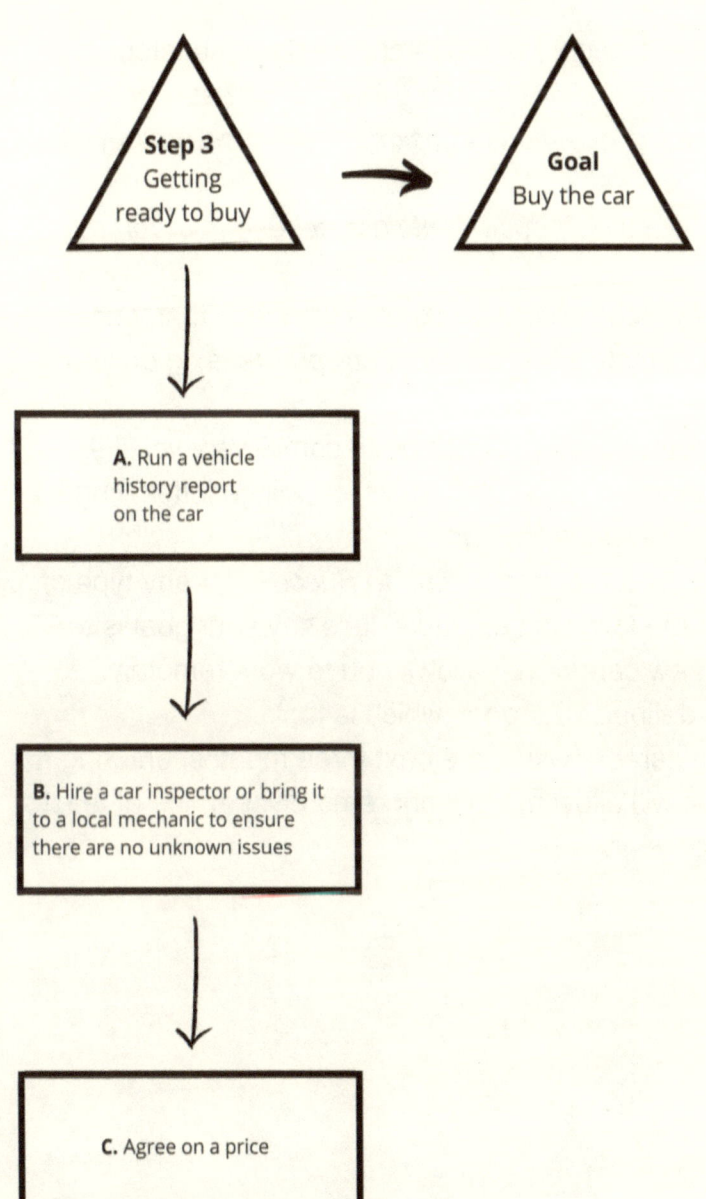

Step 3
Getting
ready to buy

Goal
Buy the car

A. Run a vehicle
history report
on the car

B. Hire a car inspector or bring it
to a local mechanic to ensure
there are no unknown issues

C. Agree on a price

Under the category of research, the three substeps are:
A. *Find a 1971 Ford Mustang Mach 1 for sale*
B. *Research questions to ask car sellers before buying a classic car*
C. *Find out which documents are needed in order to buy the car*
Each of these substeps acts as milestones that, once passed, let you know how you are progressing on your journey.

After substep, *C* has been completed, you'll then move on to the next substep, which will be letter *A* under *Step 2: Test drive the car*.

You can create a *Path to Success* for any type of goal. In the following example, let's say your goal is to start a new career that allows you to work remotely. You've defined your goal, which is to:
Change careers within the next three months, entering a field that will allow me to work remotely, earning at least $70k per year.

Path to Success Example 2

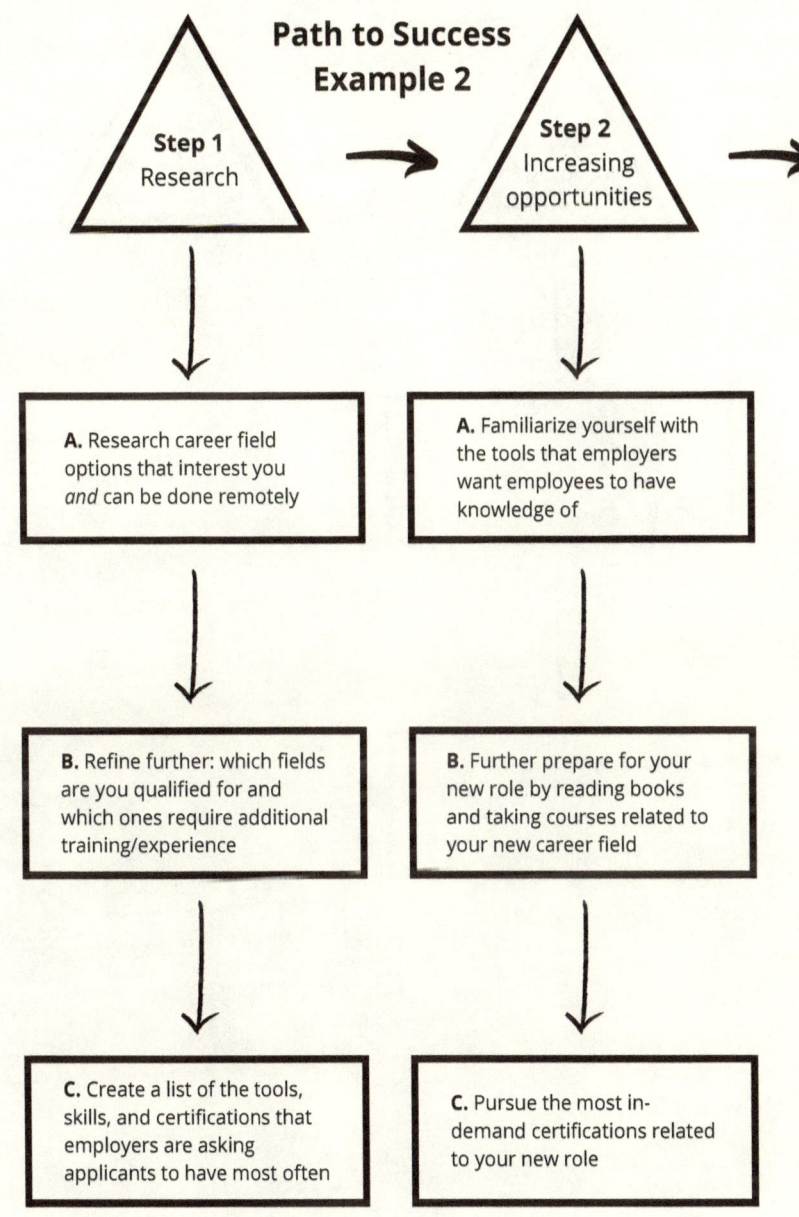

Step 1
Research

Step 2
Increasing opportunities

A. Research career field options that interest you *and* can be done remotely

A. Familiarize yourself with the tools that employers want employees to have knowledge of

B. Refine further: which fields are you qualified for and which ones require additional training/experience

B. Further prepare for your new role by reading books and taking courses related to your new career field

C. Create a list of the tools, skills, and certifications that employers are asking applicants to have most often

C. Pursue the most in-demand certifications related to your new role

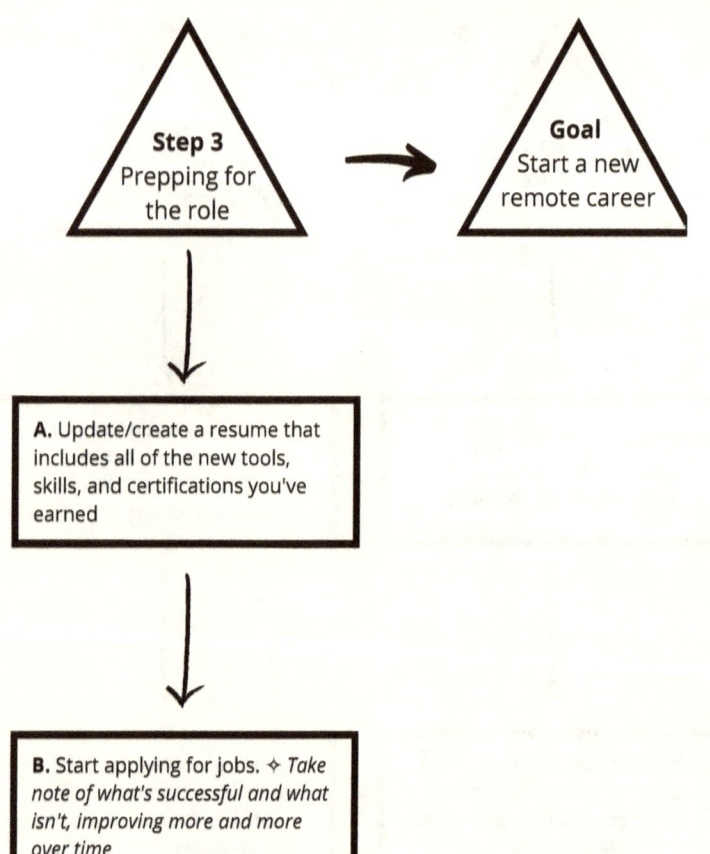

Step 3
Prepping for
the role

Goal
Start a new
remote career

A. Update/create a resume that includes all of the new tools, skills, and certifications you've earned

B. Start applying for jobs. ✦ *Take note of what's successful and what isn't, improving more and more over time*

The first step will be *Step 1* Research. You'll start by completing substep *A. Research career field options that interest you and can be done remotely.*

From there, you'll move onto substep *B. Refine further: which fields are you qualified for, and which ones require additional training/experience.*

The final steps will involve updating your current resumé/creating a new resumé, applying for jobs, and landing the role.

◆

These are examples of the types of paths you can take to get to specific destinations. But remember, there are an infinite number of paths that can lead you to your objectives. What's important here is knowing how to create a *Path to Success* for yourself. Your path will likely look different depending on what your goals are, and that's ok.

The overarching idea is to determine all of the steps you'll need to take in order to succeed, break those steps down into substeps, and then monitor your own success as you're on your journey.

You may need to make iterations to the *Path* as you're actively pursuing your goals. Those iterations may come from newly-gained knowledge or experience. If you're learning about ways of reaching your goals more quickly and efficiently, then make those updates to the *Path to Success* as needed.

What's most important is clearly defining the steps on the journey and analyzing the progress you're making along the way.

Resources

Creating a *Resource Forecast*

A *Resource Forecast* is meant to be used in conjunction with your *Path to Success*

In the previous section, you researched and established all of the steps that need to be taken in order to complete your goal. Drill down even further and find out which resources you'll need to complete each step.

The *Path to Success* tells you all of the steps you'll need to take in order to complete your goal. The *Resource Forecast* breaks those steps down and establishes the resources that are required in order to complete each step.

Let's create a *Resource Forecast* for the example of buying your dream car.

Example Resource Forecast

Step on the Path to Success	Resources required to complete each step	Resources I already have	Resources that I don't currently have	Steps to obtaining all required resources
Research	• Time • Computer or smart phone	Computer	Time, in order to conduct research	1. Determine where time is being spent currently 2. Which daily activities can be performed more efficiently 3. Remove all lower-priority tasks to make more time in the day
Test drive the car	Valid drivers license		Valid drivers license	Need to renew expired license
Getting ready to buy	Funds to buy the car	Have $7,500 to spend on car	Need another $7,500	• Move into a higher-paid position • Take on a second role temporarily • Try to work extra hours in my current role and/or get a raise

All of the steps that you established in your *Path to Success* will be listed in the first column of your *Resource Forecast*.

Under the column *Resources required to complete each step*, you'll list just that. If the first step is *Research*, then what are the resources you'll need in order to complete it? Time is one resource you'll need. Another resource would be a means of conducting the research.

Having a computer or smartphone would be the easiest way to complete this step. You can then list the two required resources that you'll need: time and a computer or smartphone.

In the next section, *Resources I already have*, you'll list the resources you currently own that will allow you to complete this step.

Do you have the time to properly conduct this research? Do you own a computer or smartphone, or do you have access to one? Let's say you have a computer, but you don't have the time. That's what the column, *Resources that I don't currently have*, is for. In this column, you'd write, "Time, in order to conduct research."

In the final column, *Steps to obtaining all required resources*, you'll outline the steps you'll need to take in order to acquire any resources you don't have, yet.

Resources You May Already Have

Depending on your goal and what it will take to achieve it, you might feel like you don't have any resources at your disposal at all. What a dismal thought! Luckily, it couldn't be further from the truth. Below are examples of resources you might have available to you right now.

As you find additional resources you may not have previously realized you had, update your *Resource Forecast* as needed.

Time

Time is your greatest resource, which is why it's so important to use it wisely. For many goals, you'll need to spend a certain amount of time on planning as an initial step. Taking the time to plan is instrumental to your success. A clear, well-defined plan will be the foundation upon which all other steps will be built.

More than any other resource, time is perhaps the most important. If you're overworked and can't take the time to check in with yourself and establish a clear goal, you might end up doing something that really doesn't provide much value to your life.

By having an adequate amount of time, you can learn a new skill, study, and achieve certifications in your desired field. Most importantly, you can use it to evaluate where you are on your journey and where you want to be.

Just for the mental clarity alone, time is invaluable. You need to give yourself that space to figure out where you are, where you're going, and what you can do to further expedite your own progress. This continuous analysis will be one of your greatest assets, as success is nearly impossible without it.

Allowing yourself the time to reflect on what your goals truly are is imperative to achieving success.

Depending on what your goal is, you may only need to dedicate 15 minutes a day to pursue it. The amount of time needed will depend on what your goals are.

You may already have the amount of time needed to start working toward achieving your goal just by rearranging some tasks in your day or by performing tasks more efficiently. Start by analyzing how much time you'll need and how much time you have available to you each day.

Knowledge & Skills

What skills or knowledge might you already have that can aid you on your journey? For example, if you want to take a well-deserved trip, your knowledge of how to find cheap airfare and your exquisite haggling skills will take you places!

If changing careers is your goal, then all of the knowledge you've already acquired since entering the workforce can be applied to the new career of your choosing.

Even if the career you want to move into is miles away from anything else you've ever done, find the similarities between what you've learned and what you will need to know when entering your new career field. Apply your previously acquired knowledge and skills to your new role.

For instance, if you're looking to get into project management, ask yourself, have you ever managed people, projects, time, or budgets in *any* capacity? Those are all relevant experiences and skills that you can apply to your new career.

If you're looking to run your own company, do you have *any* experience that could relate? Maybe you've spent most of your career helping others run their companies. While you may not have experience running your own business, you *do* have experience running businesses at a high level.

Evaluate what you've learned throughout your career and apply it to your new venture.
It's up to you to find the similarities and links between what you already know and what you need to know, but I'm sure you'll find the similarities once you start looking for them.

Money

Money is a valuable resource that could make achieving your goal easier, depending on the goal.
After researching how much money you'll need to achieve your goal, you can evaluate how much of those funds you already have.

But be sure you retain a certain amount of savings before starting to fund any goals! Even if it means taking a little extra time to finance your goal, take that time, and keep your safety net intact.

Friends and Family

Friends, family members, and loved ones are wonderful resources to have. They offer unlimited amounts of love and emotional support as well as advice, knowledge, and wisdom.

I encourage you to talk about your dreams and goals with loved ones but remember not to let anyone's negative experiences influence you. Nonetheless, you *can* use their advice as cautionary tales when appropriate.

If someone really does raise your awareness of potential risks to either your health, happiness or your goal itself, just prepare for the chance that those events may take place and hope that they don't occur. You can never be too prepared, so long as you keep moving forward.

The only time you'll encounter risks is while actively pursuing your goal. What's interesting is that even the act of preparing for potential risks is helping to make your goal more real. You're just another step closer to achieving your dreams.

Equipment

Do you have any equipment that might assist you while on your journey? You definitely do if you have a computer, laptop or smartphone. Through these devices, you have unlimited knowledge available to you at any time of the day or night. This will make it much easier to research the goals you're in the process of achieving.

Computers and smartphones are just a couple of examples of tools you might have available to you. Depending on your goal, you might need a car or hardware of some kind.

Utilize your surroundings. There are more options available to you than you might realize initially. If you keep looking for ways to achieve success, I guarantee that you will find them.

Resource Assembling

Acquiring the Resources You'll Need in Order to Achieve Your Dreams

Taking Hold of Your Time

One of the most common reasons people feel like they're not able to achieve success is because they don't have time for themselves. Isn't that a weird concept?

You're living your own life, yet, you don't have time for yourself? For the things you care most about? For the things that will bring you the most peace, joy, happiness, and satisfaction?

If that's the case, we're going to have to divide and conquer in order to find out where your time is truly being spent. Is your time being spent at a demanding job? Do you have a long commute?

You might even just have a very active social life and not realize that you don't have "time for yourself" because you're at the club every night.

I'm not here to tell you not to go to the club every night. Enjoy your life! But, if you're not happy and you're feeling ready to make a significant change in your life, then it's essential to figure out where you're spending most of your time and how you can reallocate that time towards the things you care about the most.

You'll have to decide which areas of your life you'd like to continue spending your time in and where you can make some cuts in order to free up time in your schedule to pursue your goals.

That could mean spending less time at a demanding job. It could mean spending less time online or on social media. It could mean reducing the number of stressful situations you experience on a daily basis that take both your time and your energy.

Whatever those time suckers are, now is the time to identify them and remove them from your schedule.

◆

In order to figure out how to maximize the number of hours you have to spend working towards your goals each day, you first need to determine how your time is currently being spent. You might have a general idea right now, but if you dig deeper, the results may surprise you.

Begin with tracking how much time you're spending on different activities throughout the day. Start by tracking activity times for two to three days out of the week. The easiest way to do this is by using time-tracking software.

The website Clockify.me is one of many free time tracking websites you can use. Time-tracking software works by the user typing in an activity (e.g. at work, watching T.V., reading, cleaning, etc.) then starting and stopping the timer through a mobile app or on a desktop.

If you don't have a computer or a mobile phone, you can always track your time the old-fashioned way. Break out the ol' pen and paper and repeat the same steps as above. Write down your activity, such as commuting to work, washing dishes, or cooking dinner. Then simply write down your start and end times. After tracking your time for two or three days, review the results.

When analyzing how long you spend cooking each day, washing dishes, watching T.V., or on your phone, are you starting to see possible ways of increasing the amount of time you have each day to spend on your goals? Now you have hard data on what you spend your time on, which means you can start optimizing your time and making room in your day, and your life, for what matters to you most.

There's no such thing as "I don't have time."
You have time. It's up to you how you use it.

For the activities we have to do every day, like cleaning, cooking, taking showers, exercising, and getting ready, we can't stop doing those things, nor would I recommend that. But are there ways to do these things more efficiently? Is it possible to do these activities in a way where they're not as time-consuming?

For example, if you find that you're spending one full day cleaning every week, might it be easier to instead, spend 15-30 minutes cleaning each day, instead of spending an entire day on cleaning alone?

If you live with other people, don't be scared to ask them to help clean as well. You might feel like no one will clean quite as well as you do, but your approach to cleaning can be taught, I promise. Give others chances to show you that they can help, too. Consider dividing larger tasks into smaller tasks that you can perform during the week.

If you're noticing that you're spending hours cooking every day, try researching quick, easy, and healthy recipes that can be made in 30 minutes or less. You can also cook in bulk and freeze the leftovers, which will help save you time in the long run. Wherever your time is being spent, start considering why those activities are taking as long as they are and how you can reduce that time.

Phone Time

When you start tracking your time, you might be shocked to find out just how much time you're spending on your phone every day. So many of us wake up, grab our phones, and proceed to spend 20 or 30 minutes on them, sometimes before we even get out of bed in the morning. Before we go to sleep, the last thing we do is cruise the news or social media channels, and a few minutes, or hours later, we go to sleep.

These are habits, and although you may enjoy your phone time when first waking up or before going to sleep, what's more important? 1 to 3 hours of phone time a day or spending 1 to 3 hours achieving your goals and living your dream life?

Setting your phone to, "airplane mode," is a feature on mobile phones that prevents the phone from receiving calls or using the internet. The, "do not disturb," option on phones allows you to control a bit more such as, whether or not you'll allow phone calls to come in, text messages, or other alerts.

Utilizing either of these options are just some of the ways you can reduce phone time. They both create barriers for yourself, making it slightly more difficult to just pick up your phone and start surfing the internet.

Another way to reduce your phone time is to replace the time you'd typically spend on your phone with another activity that's more productive and fulfilling and, ideally, something related to your goal.

Reading a book before going to sleep is one way to spend more time on something that could bring you closer to your goal. Another could be practicing an instrument, exercising, or even just spending quality time with a loved one.

Instead of using your phone, spend some time before bed to reflect on how the day went. Ask yourself what went well, and what you would like to accomplish the next day.

Daily check-ins with yourself will help you acknowledge the progress you made that day, and will also give you a plan for the following day.
By checking in with yourself, you're another step closer to your goal.

Another option is to allow yourself to spend time on your phone, but only during specific times of the day. For example, as your coffee is brewing in the morning, you can tell yourself that you'll only use your phone until your coffee is ready.

Give yourself that time to watch funny videos, check out social media channels, or catch up on the news. But, when the coffee is ready, put the phone down and carry on with your day.

When you first start pursuing a goal, you especially need to become more conscious of your time. Managing your time very closely will help you advance on your journey much more quickly. You'll end up spending more time on the things that you care about and less time on the things that provide little to no value to your life.

◆

Maybe your phone is constantly receiving notifications from games, apps, or email boxes? You probably pick up your phone when it makes a *ding* to see what you're being notified of. Now is the time to reduce the number of distractions to the bare minimum.

Consider turning off your notifications. After all, what do you really *need* to be notified about in real-time? Phone calls, messages, maybe email, but most likely not even email, unless you're waiting for an important email, which in my experience, is rare. Reduce the amount of distractions and focus on the things that will benefit you the most.

Taking Your Time Back from Your Job

If you find yourself constantly thinking about work while you're not there, consider this: when you're mentally at work, you're at work. The only difference is, you're not getting paid for that additional time.

You're at work when you wake up in the morning and start commiserating over your ever-growing to-do list, scheduled meetings, and how you're going to manage it all.

When you get home on a weekday, work might be on your mind for 1 to 3 hours. Let's say two. Weekends are no exception, and work creeps back into your mind for about three hours between Saturday and Sunday, especially Sunday when you start dreading doing it all over again the next day.

Let's look at this equation:

13 hours of thinking about your job every week

x 4 weeks per month

= 52 hours per month

Those are 52 hours, every month, spent mentally at work, without being compensated for the extra time you're putting in!

When you're thinking about work, you're at work. You're not on vacation. You're not enjoying the weekend. You're not having breakfast with the family or having drinks with friends. This is a bad habit, but one that you can break today. Take your time back from your job and instead give it to the things, moments and people that matter to you most.

Shift your focus and retrain your brain. Say to yourself, "Every time I catch myself thinking about work, I'm going to instead start thinking about my goal, immediately! No ifs, ands, or buts about it. My job is only stressing me out and I'm not going to give it any more time than I already have."

An empowering mantra like this, when carried out over and over again, will help you take control of your time and your mind. Now, you'll have 52 extra hours every month to spend thinking about your goals instead!

Maybe you'll use that time to pontificate on how excited you'll be once you've completed your goals and also ways that you can accomplish them sooner. These are the best thoughts to have.

You may start to notice that you're feeling lighter and even more energized throughout the day—run with those feelings and keep doing more of the things that you love!

Stop Working Nights & Weekends

Let's say that, when you leave work, you forget all about it and never give it another thought. Great to hear! But, unfortunately, you have a job that emails you at all hours of the day and expects you to work nights and weekends.

Does something always seem to come up right before the clock strikes 5 p.m. on a Friday? Maybe you're getting paid for the extra hours worked, but perhaps you're not. But, even if you are, is this how you want to spend your time and life?

Don't feel bad. It's happened to the best of us. Especially when you start working at a new job and want to keep that job, so when your boss casually asks if you can work on something outside of regular business hours, you oblige.

Unfortunately, you've just set the precedent for the rest of your time with that company. If you accept *some* work outside of what's part of your job description, it's likely that you'll be willing to do *more* work when asked.

Slowly, the emails start trickling in past regular business hours. Over time, it becomes expected that you'll work extra hours and will be available nights and weekends. So, now that this is the expectation, how do you take charge of your time and subsequently your life? If you are a new employee, it is vital that you set the precedent for what you deem acceptable and unacceptable, as early on as possible.

The first step is signaling to the team and the company the hours of the day that you're going to be "working" which, for most people, will be between the hours of 9 a.m. and 5 p.m.

Many companies use communication tools, such as *Slack* and *Google Chat* when talking to other team members. Set your communication tools to "Do Not Disturb," or, "Away," when you're off the clock.

Now the part that's even more challenging — don't ever open up work emails or communication platforms when you're not at work. There are no exceptions. Just don't do it. You're not at work, and you're not getting paid any extra for being available all the time. So, why are you doing it? Are you trying to be nice? Maybe you're just trying to keep your job.

Whatever the case may be, they'll most likely respect you more for defining boundaries and valuing your own time. Setting healthy boundaries shows that you're a professional and you aren't desperate. You're not willing to accept unfair arrangements in order to keep your job because you know your worth.

You are, however, willing to work hard, produce high-quality results, and ensure you're present and a contributing member of the team. But, working all hours of the night and on weekends was never part of the deal, nor should it be.

If employers want to offer you additional compensation for being more available, and if this is acceptable to you, then that's fine. But remember, you don't have an infinite number of hours in the day or in your life.

How you spend your time matters so spend it wisely. Besides, how will you ever reach your *own* goals if you're always working around the clock for someone else?

Time is your greatest asset.
It's yours to give away, and it's yours to take back.

Now, how do you get out of working nights and weekends if you've already been working these extra hours for some time? There are a few ways. The first is, to tell the truth.

If your job sends you emails incessantly, and if the team already knows you to be an employee that's always responsive, then let the team know some things in your personal life have changed, and you will only be able to respond to emails and messages during 9 a.m. and 5 p.m., or whenever your working hours are.

The thing that changed in your personal life was you taking charge of your time and prioritizing your goals above a transitory job. Your boss may reply with, "But, we need you...Who will take care of...? You're the only one who knows how to..."
If your boss is unhappy with this change and starts digging deeper, "What's changed in your life?" then a simple, non-confrontational reply of, "It's personal," is more than sufficient and will end the interrogation promptly.

If your boss needs someone on call nights and weekends, then they will have to hire additional team members to work nights and weekends — bottom line.

If you are the only team member who knows how something works, then change that. Teach what you know to others or offer to train any new hires so they're up to speed as quickly as possible.

This approach can stop communication outside of regular working hours, and it can also block your boss from asking you to come into the office on the weekend, especially if you haven't been getting compensated for it.

Eliminate Your Daily Commute Entirely

You might expect the following suggestions to include relocating in order to be closer to your job, but that's probably not something you want to do, and why would you?

Uprooting your entire life is a massive commitment. It can involve potentially spending more money on rent or on a mortgage, and when you consider the high level of uncertainty in the workforce, who's to say you'll even be at the same job in just a year or two? Luckily, moving closer to work isn't the only option you have for eliminating your daily commute.

There are lots of ways you're able to put an end to commuting. One way is by working remotely. Remote jobs are jobs that can be performed from home. Remote work is becoming increasingly popular. Many remote companies pay as much as on-site jobs. They also include many of the same benefits, such as healthcare, 401k plans, and life insurance. But, what they offer goes much further than financial benefits alone. Working remotely increases your time, peace of mind, and quality of life.

Remote work allows you to put an end to worrying about waking up at the crack of dawn in order to beat rush hour traffic. Your diet can improve while working from home since you won't be subjected to eating at whichever fast-food restaurant just happens to be within walking distance of your job. You'll get more done and will be able to spend more time with the people and pets you love the most. You'll even save money on clothes for work since most remote employers take a more casual approach to their dress codes.

These are just some of the many benefits of working remotely. So, how do you find remote work opportunities?

Working Remotely

Let's say you only have basic computer skills and you've never worked for a company that was fully remote before. You're interested in working remotely, but you aren't sure how to get started.

There are some occupations, such as bartending, waitressing, landscaping, and construction that have to be done on-site. If you're serious about change, you may need to leave the field you're in, if working remotely in your current role isn't an option.

The first step will be to figure out which career fields interest you the most and what you're the most qualified to do right now. You can even focus on finding a job that relates to other goals you have, which would make achieving those goals easier.

For example, if your primary goal is to be a photographer, then working remotely as a photo editor would be a job that would relate to your primary goal.

The best way to enter a new remote field is by starting out in an entry-level position. A great way to find these positions is by visiting a job search engine such as, Indeed.com or Linkedin.com, searching for *entry-level positions* that are also *remote*. As you're searching for these positions, review the job postings, and start seriously considering any roles that you're currently capable of performing and roles that you might even be good at.

I recommend avoiding commission-based roles since there's no certainty that you will make any money at all. Also, many of them offer fewer benefits than salaried positions. You'll also want to avoid any job postings that ask for sensitive information or require you to pay, even a small fee, in order to get started. These are likely scams and should be avoided at all costs.

Perform research on companies before applying. You can find reviews for many companies, left by current and past employees. These will give you further insight as to whether or not this role will be a good fit. Stick with salaried or hourly positions. They exist and many of them offer everything on-site jobs do, such as health care, dental, vision, life insurance, vacation time, paid holidays and sick leave. Some companies even pay their employees a full day's salary for time spent volunteering.

It's almost unbelievable that there are so many remote work options available, offering the same benefits that on-site jobs offer, but without the commute or the need to live in a specific location in order to work with the company.

Acquiring More Knowledge and Skills

Depending on what your goals are, you might need to learn new skills or gain knowledge in unfamiliar areas. There are lots of avenues to go down in order to expand your skill set and increase your knowledge. Let's start with the basics.

✧ *For any skills that don't apply to you, feel free to skip ahead!*

Learn Basic Computer Skills

The amount of research you're able to conduct by having access to the internet is astounding. In today's digital age, utilizing free resources on the internet will open up a world of possibilities such as the ability to work remotely, not to mention the sheer amount of knowledge you'll have available right at your fingertips.

If you don't know how to use a computer, you can take free adult education classes on learning basic computer skills. These classes are available for free through public libraries, both virtually and onsite.

For example, below, you'll find a link to the *New York Public Library* website where they offer free on-site and virtual continuing education courses. Nypl.org/events/classes/calendar

The *New York Public Library* also offers free classes on learning how to code and how to use popular software such as *Excel, Adobe Photoshop, Word, PowerPoint* and more. This is just one of many available resources. Do your research and never be scared to ask for help.

Breaking Into a New Career

One of the best ways to enter a new career field is by examining the tools, skills, and certifications that employers are asking for the most in job postings. Then make a plan that includes studying and receiving those certifications while learning new skill sets and tools.

Start by reviewing active job listings on job search engines, such as Indeed.com. Then create lists of the skills, tools and certifications that different job postings ask for in your chosen field. You can even write a number next to each one to represent the amount of times you've seen specific skills, tools, or certifications mentioned.

If you find that there are a lot of job postings asking applicants to have a working knowledge of a tool like *Adobe Photoshop,* for example, then seek out ways of acquainting yourself with that software. Most software offers free trials or may even be free to use or download. While a week or a month on a free trial may not make you an expert, it might be just enough time to give you a basic understanding of how that software works.

If you spend a lot of time during your free trial studying the software and watching tutorials online, then you'll be able to speak about your experience with that program more confidently during interviews. This approach can be used for any field in any salary range.

Getting Certified

If there are certifications you're noticing employers are asking for, perform an internet search for ways of attaining those certifications. Many certifications are free, but they can take time to complete. Some can be attained in a day, while others could take weeks or months to earn.

You'll have to weigh out the pros and cons of receiving specific certifications. If you don't know where to start and want to ensure that you're pursuing certifications from accredited organizations that will impress employers the most, all you'll have to do is perform a bit of research.

Searching for answers to your questions on discussion websites can be an excellent option for getting answers from real people, as well as learning new and interesting information on various topics.

Reddit, at Reddit.com*, and Quora at* Quora.com are popular online discussion websites, but remember you never want to only follow one source's advice, so be sure to get your information from a variety of places.

These are just some of the ways to get started in a new career field. Remember, never stop learning! Even if you have interviews that don't go well, take something from them. What did you learn? What questions did the employer ask of you? How can you better prepare for the next one? It's likely that those same questions will pop up in future interviews in the same field. So, if you didn't know the answers during the interview, find out what those answers are and arm yourself with knowledge for your next interview.

Keep improving and keep learning. Don't be afraid to make mistakes, just be sure to learn from them and take that knowledge with you as you move forward. Below are some useful websites that offer certifications in popular fields.

Coursera, at Coursera.org, offers free educational courses online, in addition to paid courses where certifications can be earned. You can receive certifications, and degrees, from world-class universities in fields ranging from computer science and information technology to social sciences, math, and business.

You can take free online courses and receive certifications for *Google* platforms such as *Google Ads, Google Analytics,* and *Google My Business* by visiting *Google Skillshop,* at Skillshop.withgoogle.com

If you'd like to get certified in *Excel, PowerPoint,* or *Microsoft 365,* you can do so by visiting Docs.microsoft.com/en-us/learn/certifications

Do your research and find out which certifications will benefit you the most—then get certified. Be sure to add your newly acquired certifications to your resumé and don't be shy about bringing them up during interviews. They will help give potential employers more faith in your skills and experience.

Books, Ebooks and Audio Books

If you're looking to learn more on a particular subject but aren't sure where to start or which books would be the most beneficial to read, start by performing an internet search for, "The best books for learning how to..." and explore the books other people have found to be helpful.

Do you see the same books coming up over and over again? Carry on with your research and read reviews on the books you're most interested in. You might also be able to view the Table of Contents and some pages in the book before purchasing. Make sure the books are relevant to the topic you're studying and at your skill level, be it beginner, intermediate, or expert.

Amazon, at Amazon.com, is an online retail website that has a wide selection of hardcover, Ebooks, and audiobooks. Ebooks are often less expensive than hardcover books. Two popular online audiobook platforms are Audible, at Audible.com, and Google Audiobooks, which can be accessed through the downloadable app, Google Play Books & Audiobooks.

A great online bookseller, ThriftBooks, at Thriftbooks.com, offers an extensive selection of affordable new and used books. They also have an incredible selection of affordable textbooks, so if you're looking to expand your knowledge and expertise, this could be a great resource.

Be sure to choose books that you'll genuinely enjoy reading. I recommend buying one book at a time since your needs can change based on what's covered in that book. When you're close to finishing that book, you can move on to the next one.

Online Course Websites

In addition to the research you're conducting and the books you're reading, you may want to take an online course as well. I'll go over my favorite online course websites and what makes each one so unique.

My number one choice for continuing education online is *edX* at, Edx.org, which is a global nonprofit founded by Harvard and MIT.

EdX offers free educational courses on a variety of subjects. *EdX* is an excellent resource for continuing education professionally and personally.

LinkedIn Learning, at Linkedin.com/learning, is another excellent platform offering courses on monthly subscription plans. They are a great resource for continuing education, specifically in creative fields, such as photography and graphic design. They also have courses on web development, software development, and business. *Udemy*, at Udemy.com, offers courses ranging from photography and IT to productivity, web development, marketing, finance, and academics. Course prices vary, but most courses cost around $15.

I highly recommend reading reviews before signing up for courses. Reviews are left by students who have already taken the course. Many reviews offer helpful insights, such as how participants felt about the course, what the course focused on from their perspectives, and what they learned.

Earning More Money

Do you need a certain amount of money in order to accomplish your goal? If you do, you'll want to establish how much you have, how much you'll need, and how you're going to acquire additional funds.

You may have a chance of working overtime or receiving a raise in your current role.

Will working overtime provide enough additional revenue to help you reach your goal and if so, how much overtime would you need to work and for how long? If a raise will soon become available to you, will that raise give you enough extra earnings to fund your goal?

If either of those are viable options, do the math and plan accordingly. However, if neither of those options are available *or* if they wouldn't provide the income needed, then you'll have to seek out other options.

It's not about penny-pinching, it's about money-earning. If you need the kind of money that, let's face it, so many of us do, then you're going to have to think big and break out of your comfort zone.

If you want different results,
you have to perform different actions.

That could mean entering into a new career field, starting your own business, or earning a living from your talents, despite how scary or intimidating those paths may sound.

So many jobs are designed to keep us on that spinning wheel. Never giving us exactly what we need, so we *have to* keep coming back day after day, after day, hoping that our dreams will somehow come true and the cycle will end.

How you spend your time
is how you spend your life.

Do you want to start each day looking forward to the day ending quickly, just so you can go home and do it over again the next day, or do you want to live a life where you enjoy every moment, hoping that the days never end?

There are a million ways to earn the amount of money that you'll need in order to turn your dreams into realities. Let's explore some.

Working Remotely

The reason I'm listing this first isn't because you'll necessarily become a millionaire working remotely, but, working remotely can allow you to double your income in a very short period of time. Depending on what your financial goals are, that boost in revenue could be precisely what you need in order to achieve success.

When you work from home, you eliminate your daily commute entirely as we covered, but this is just the beginning of the many ways you can increase your income when working remotely.

Being in a remote role opens up the possibility of taking on multiple, low-demanding roles. This can be tricky, but manageable, and if you're willing to put in the time, you can double your income reasonably quickly.

You'll have to figure out your ideal work-life structure, how much time you're willing to spend working every day, and how much money you need to save before leaving one or both positions. You should also be aware of any meeting times that could conflict between roles, but if you structure things well, there won't be any issues.

As I said, this isn't the way to become a millionaire, but it's listed here first because, by doubling your income, you might be able to fund your own business ventures or perhaps your goal only requires a small amount of money you don't currently have. If that's the case doubling up on work would be temporary and might be enough to help you reach your destination.

Put yourself on a financial plan that includes an end date to you working both jobs. If you work for two companies for too long, you're at risk of burnout. The doubling of work should just be a *temporary solution*.

✦ Bonus! If you have any interest in traveling and want to save the maximum amount of money possible, you can always relocate to a less expensive city, state, or country, earning the same amount of money as if you were living in a more expensive city.

When you start researching other cities, states, or countries and what the cost of living is, the reality may shock you. Just be aware of the time zone difference between where your jobs are located and where you are.

Starting Your Own Business

All great businesses began by having one of two things. Either a unique idea or a major improvement on an already existing idea.

Before innovators and thought leaders held those titles, they were just people with ideas. They found gaps in the market, possible ways for them to turn their business ideas into viable sources of income, and they acted on those ideas.

I know it's much easier to get a job and stay at that job than it is to create a business from scratch. But it is possible, and that proof is all around us.

Start considering, what are we missing as a society? What tools can businesses benefit from that would significantly increase their productivity? What can people use that will improve quality of life around the world?

Starting your own business can come in many forms. It can be a professional business that will employ hundreds of people, or it can be earning a living through creative talents, such as writing, acting, singing, directing, sculpting or any other creative pursuit.

The point is that you're earning a living on your own, that's not dependent on an employer. Instead, you're the person creating your own opportunities, without there being a cap on your salary.

When you start running your own business, you'll quickly start looking at salaried positions differently.

Those salaries you once dreamed of earning are now looked at as limiting since there's a ceiling to your earnings. When you make a living independent of any single employer, there's no cap on how much you can earn. Your earning potential becomes limitless.

A tremendously helpful resource for prospective business owners in America is the *U.S. Small Business Administration,* at Sba.gov.

They offer an abundance of free business resources and can answer many questions that you may have about starting a business.

SCORE, at Score.org offers remote mentoring for prospective business owners and anyone who has business-related questions. Their mentorship program is made up of volunteer business mentors who can guide you through the process of starting a business. From the About Us page on the *SCORE* website, "Since 1964, we have provided education and mentorship to more than 11 million entrepreneurs."[7]

I highly recommend finding answers to your questions through the *U.S. Small Business Administration* website or by reaching out to the real-life mentors at *SCORE* who are here to help.

---

[7] SCORE. SCORE: Homepage.

Make a Living off Your Expertise

What are you an expert in? You might not consider yourself an expert in anything, so, how about this, what are some things you're really good at? Maybe you've been working in a specific field for many years. I'm sure you've learned a lot about how to perform that job and how to do it incredibly well.

Can you provide guidance for anyone else wanting to enter that field? Is there anything you wish you had known before starting work in that role? What are the most important things you've learned thus far? Start asking yourself these questions.

Maybe you're an artist and you love doing make-up, cooking or crocheting. Ask yourself the same questions. This can be applied to anyone, in any field. Offer the knowledge you've acquired to other people. You'll be shocked to find out that people might really benefit from your teachings.

So, how do you make a living off your expertise? One way is to create a website and sell online products/services there. This route could take a bit of time and might have a startup fee if you're paying a company to build a website for you. However, the upside is that you'd receive all of the profits from the offerings you sell.

There are inexpensive ways to build and launch websites these days. *Squarespace*, at Squarespace.com is a great option for most small business owners, and it comes with a relatively small price tag compared to paying a company to build you a website from scratch.

However, if you're an e-commerce business and are selling products online, *Shopify*, at Shopify.com might be a better fit. If you sell handmade products, you could also sell your products on *Etsy* at Etsy.com, which is one of the largest online platforms for handmade items.

If you're interested in creating and selling online courses, you could build a website and market it on your own, but a faster way of earning money from online courses would be by posting your course to an already established online learning platform.

Online learning platforms have different ways of compensating their contributors, so be sure to review the terms first, then decide which platform is right for you. *Udemy*, at Udemy.com has really grown in popularity and is one of the most widely used online learning platforms currently. *Udemy* offers courses in almost every subject you can think of. From health and fitness to music, finance, personal development, marketing, design, and more.

Skillshare, at Skillshare.com is a popular online learning platform that enables users of the platform to teach classes in fields such as, illustration and music, as well as business, lifestyle, productivity, and web development to name a few.

Maybe writing is your forte. If it is, you can write an Ebook, a hardcover book, create an audiobook, or all of the above.

There are lots of ways of getting the word out. You'll have to decide what makes the most sense, based on the area you're an expert in and which platforms your target audience uses most.

Tracking Your Finances

No matter how much money you have or don't have, you always need to know how much money is coming in, from which sources, and where your money is being spent. If you don't take the time to figure this out, you'll never have a firm grasp over your finances.

The tool that I recommend using to keep track of your finances is *Mint*. It's a free, easy-to-use app that's available on both desktop and mobile devices. *Mint*, at Mint.intuit.com, is a budgeting tool created by the makers of *QuickBooks* and *TurboTax*, which allows you to link up all of your financial accounts in one place and then look at your spending and overall finances from a higher level.

If you want to look at your spending more closely and don't mind it being a more manual process, I would recommend using a spreadsheet.

Google Sheets, at Docs.google.com/spreadsheets, is a free spreadsheet program that even offers a *Monthly Budgeting* template. This template allows you to take a more granular look at your finances.

The only downside is that you do need to plug information into the spreadsheet manually, which is more laborious and time-consuming than using a tool like *Mint* which pulls the data automatically.

Regardless of whether you're using *Mint* or a *Google Sheet,* it's a good practice to examine your debit and credit card statements at least monthly.
By analyzing your finances, you'll increase awareness of your expenditure as well as which sources are producing the most income.

Assembling a Team & Getting Work Done

Hiring Employees & Independent Contractors

Depending on your goal, you may need to get a team together or hire a company to assist you with work that will need to be completed. Before doing any research on individuals or companies, you'll want to start with the people you already know who you believe would make great team members.

Knowing someone who has the skills that you need in order to help you reach your goal is usually preferred. This is because you already know the person, know how reliable they are, and what they're capable of taking on. If you don't know anyone who's able to help, then you'll need to assemble externally. Below are some resources that will help you find qualified candidates.

Indeed, offers free job postings as well as paid sponsored ads, which help get your job listing in the line of sight of more candidates. It's great for people searching for employees or contractors for short-term projects or long-term employment.

LinkedIn, at Linkedin.com, is another great website for posting jobs. *LinkedIn* is a platform for professionals, consisting of over, "...800 million members..."[8] You can post a job listing for free or run paid ads.

If you're looking for creative work to be carried out, *Behance*, at Behance.net, is a great website to post a job listing to. You can discover talented artists on *Behance* who may be perfect for creative work that needs to be carried out including, graphic design, photography and photo-editing projects.

Before hiring an employee or an independent contractor there are some things you'll want to think about. For instance, the line of work you're in may require all hires to sign a Non-Disclosure Agreement (NDA). Non-Disclosure Agreements restrict classified and sensitive information from being made public by anyone who signs. You'll be protecting yourself and your business by including the signing of an NDA into your onboarding process for new hires, whether they're employees or independent contractors.

---

[8] LinkedIn. About LinkedIn.

You'll also want to draw up a document that clearly states all duties and responsibilities of the person you're hiring and their compensation. If the individual will be receiving any benefits, you'll want to include those as well. Be sure to make the job description, compensation for work completed, and benefits as straightforward as possible. If there are any time frames by which the work needs to be completed, include those as well.

Communicating clearly early on will strengthen the relationships you have with the team you're building and can decrease the chances of misunderstandings taking place.

Teaming Up with Another Company

You may need to hire a company to build you a website, manufacture goods, or assist with advertising needs. For this, the greatest resource you have available to you is the internet. Once you start researching companies and feel like you've found one you'd like to work with, search for reviews of that company.

Perform an internet search for, "[company name] reviews." If you're not finding anything, try to find their *Google My Business Listing,* which should come up by typing the business's name and location while performing a search on *Google.* If the company has a *Facebook* page, you can read reviews there as well.

Before working with *any* company, you'll want to make sure you're 100% certain of all the work they will be assuming responsibility for and the time frame that work will be completed in.

Don't be afraid to ask the company to send you examples of projects they've completed previously that are similar to the work you're looking to have done. Be sure to get quotes from multiple companies before signing on the dotted line. You want to make sure you're not being overcharged or undercharged.

Paying less is great, but you don't want the work to reflect that. A company charging too little could be a sign that they're not as experienced as other companies.

However, if they can show you examples of the type of work they'll be doing for you and you're happy with the quality of that work, then it could be a mutually beneficial partnership.

Everyone has to start somewhere and sometimes when working with a smaller company you'll receive an even higher quality of work and customer service since you're not just a number to them. Weigh the pros and the cons, but remember to do your research in order to make an informed decision.

Risks & How to Reduce Them

Creating Your RAM Table

Risks can come in many forms, but being able to foresee risks can help you to avoid them. Some risks that could hinder your progress can be a lack of time, money or energy. Other risks could include feeling unmotivated, being a perfectionist or getting stuck in planning mode. These are all risks to your success, but luckily, you have a great deal of control over many of them.

Let's use our example goal of wanting to purchase a 1971 Ford Mustang Mach 1. The first step in risk mitigation is risk assessment. For that, we're going to create a *RAM (Risk Assessment and Mitigation) Table*. Your *RAM Table* is going to help you foresee potential risks at different stages of your journey before they arise. It will also help in ascertaining how severe/detrimental risks can truly be, and how likely they are to occur. Having this extra knowledge will allow you to plan accordingly.

In the first column of your *RAM Table*, you'll be listing the same steps of the journey that are listed in the *Path to Success* that you created previously.

The second column, *Potential risks*, is just that. It will detail any possible issues that may arise.

The purpose of the third column, *Risk severity*, is to assess how concerned you should be about that risk turning into a reality using a scale of 1 to 10. Give each risk a rating from 1 to 10, stating how severe/damaging the risk would be towards you completing your goal if that risk were to occur.
For example, 10 would be the most severe, meaning the most disruptive.

The fourth column, *Risk likelihood, is* where you'll be determining the probability of each risk happening. You will also use the same 1 to10 rating. 10 represents a very high chance of that risk-taking place. You might find that while going through this process, there are some risks you don't have to worry about that much, while others, you may need to prepare for.

In the final column, *How to mitigate risks*, you'll include your action plan for decreasing the chances of risks arising and/or eliminate those risks entirely. There are real risks out there, but you can improve your chances of succeeding by foreseeing them early on and taking pre-emptive measures to reduce their likelihood of occurring.

Example RAM (Risk Assessment and Mitigation) Table

Step on the Path to Success	Potential risks	Risk severity	Risk likelihood	How to mitigate risks
Research	My dream car not being available for sale in the city where I live	2	3	If I have to drive further to test drive and pick up the car, that'll be inconvenient, but manageable
Test drive the car	My drivers license is in the process of being renewed. It might not be valid by the time I'm ready to test drive the car	2	5	If needed, my friend can test drive the car for me, as I drive along in the passenger seat
Getting ready to buy	I might not be able to secure funds by the time I'm ready to buy the car	10	2	I almost have all the money needed, but if I'm not able to secure the necessary funds I will try to: 1. Find the same car at a lower cost 2. Do extra freelancing and/or consulting work 3. Watch my spending more closely

How to Foresee Potential Risks

Some of the ways to anticipate certain risks before they take place is by conducting research and utilizing free online resources such as articles, videos and discussion boards. By proactively searching for complications and obstacles that can present themselves at different stages of your journey, you're preparing yourself for the worst-case scenarios while hoping for the best.

There are many external risk factors to be aware of, but there are also internal factors that can be equally, if not more, detrimental to your success.
When we grant disapproval or negativity access into our conscience, allowing it to alter our principles or path in life, we risk not achieving our goals.

By starting to question what's possible and what we're capable of, based on fundamentally false assumptions, we're risking not having the faith in ourselves that we need in order to succeed. When we hold on to negative events from the past, we're inhibiting an improved future from turning into a reality.

If you believe you may be a potential risk to your own success, then establish lines of defense that will stop you from jeopardizing the success of your own journey. Below you'll find common risks, along with steps you can take to help reduce them.

✧ *Be sure to add any of the below risks to your RAM Table as needed.*

Common Risks and How to Mitigate Them

Feeling Unmotivated

There can be many reasons for having a lack of motivation. Is it sheer exhaustion? Are you unmotivated because you don't believe you can reach your goals, or is it because maybe the goals you've set for yourself aren't your actual goals?

Perhaps, they're not powerful enough to give you the energy you need to push forward.

> *Take this time to really assess who you are, what you want, and what's holding you back.*

Let's say the goals you have right now *are* actually ones that you're really excited about and ones that you'd like to see come true. You might be feeling a lack of motivation because you're just physically and mentally drained from your job, or other stresses in life.

> *Rid your life of time wasters and energy drainers. Make room for growth, positivity, and change.*

Reducing those stresses and replacing them with positivity, strength, motivation, and ambition will rewire

your brain and might give you the jolt of energy you
need.

It takes time to learn new habits,
but small steps create big change.

By making minor adjustments to your everyday life and
thought processes, you'll break habits that weren't
serving you and instead, replace them with the actions
that you need to take in order to turn your dreams into
realities.

Your mind can play tricks on you if it wants things
to stay the same, which it usually does. Even if the same
is making you desperately unhappy. Repetition, in this
case, also known as habits, require less mental energy,
which is why habits can feel effortless to carry out.

This is great when you have positive habits, but when
you're trying to break bad habits and form new ones,
that's when you'll experience some pushback.

You've experienced it before. When you know you're
supposed to do something and then the flood of
legitimate, but equally deceptive, excuses roll into our
psyche.

It can be from something as simple as brushing
your teeth at night to something as big as pursuing your

goal of being a professional actor, astronaut, teacher, magician, writer, artist or world traveler.

Detach yourself from the thoughts that trick you into *not* doing the things that will improve your life. Acknowledge thoughts like those, recognize they're there, and then realize that it's your scared brain trying to get out of making a change.

What the true causes of those fears might be, you'll need to figure out for yourself. Once you do, you'll be able to better manage those thoughts and feelings. Start seeing them for what they are—excuses. Reasons not to do something that are born out of fear, boredom, or fatigue.

You have the ability to recognize excuses, acknowledge their presence, and push right past them. The more you do, the fewer excuses you'll have, and the more you'll achieve.

Maybe your regular routine is getting home from work feeling beaten down, ordering a pizza, turning on the T.V. and not turning it off until you go to sleep, just to wake up again, not even one step closer to achieving your goals.

Now, it's perfectly alright to veg out, but you have goals to achieve. So, you're going to have to start reprioritizing.

*What's one small thing you can do when you get home
that will make you feel great about how you're spending
your time, while also bringing you closer to your goal?*

Only you have that exact answer, but it's about altering
your perspective, gradually. Instead of doing something
when you get home that won't help you reach your goals,
try doing something that will.

The difference is that the new action won't just
make you feel good in the moment, but it will make you
feel good in the long run, while also having a lasting
effect on your life by bringing you closer to your dreams.

If you want to make a change, take actionable
steps that will get you there and leave the excuses in the
past, where they belong.

*Your future is bright, and it's always
just one choice away.*

*Make sure the choices you make
are ones that will create positive change.*

Being Too Tired or Depressed

Being too tired to work on the things you care about is
not uncommon. Especially, when you have a long
commute for your job, are under varying degrees of
stress for 8 to 10 hours a day or spend the majority of the

workday standing or being otherwise physically active. The kids could be wearing you out or maybe you're taking care of a loved one which is taking a lot of your time and energy.

Remember, many things could affect energy levels: depression, mood, pregnancy, and illness to name a few. So, it's best to rule these out first. A simple way would be to schedule a visit with your doctor to go over the symptoms you've been experiencing.

Assuming you don't have any physical conditions that may be affecting your energy levels or mood, you're going to have to start asking yourself how you really feel about certain aspects of your life, in order to figure out which areas are bringing you down the most.

The parts of your life that are bringing you down are the first areas that will need to be changed in some way.

There are fluctuating rates of change that can occur in our lives. Some are massive changes, like moving to a new city or changing careers, other changes are more subtle, but can still have a significant impact on mood and energy levels.

Your goal might be to make a massive change, but consider what small changes you can make day-to-day that could improve your life and bring you closer to achieving success.

If you're too tired to change your life, but you're tired because you want to change your life, you're caught in a vicious circle. You may not honestly believe that you *can* accomplish your goals. If you did really believe it, you'd have enough energy to power a small country for a month!

If you *knew* that change was just a day, week, or month away, you wouldn't feel tired or run down. Instead, you'd be ecstatic, deliriously happy that your dreams were finally turning into realities.

Bottom line, if you genuinely believed that you could accomplish your goals, you wouldn't feel beaten down. You'd be energized and ready to start living your new life.

Doing research on people who come from similar backgrounds and have achieved their own dreams is something I'd especially encourage you to do.

✧ *Jump to the chapter, Success from Humble Beginnings, when you need an extra boost of motivation!*

Start planning for success by making room in your life for success to enter it.

This isn't a pep talk, it's real talk. We don't do anything in life without seeing it in our mind and planning for it before turning it into a reality.

Eating, going to work, hanging out with friends—you think about doing all of these things first, and then you carry out those actions. Goals and dreams aren't any different.

Look in the mirror and see your
ideal self staring back at you.

Maybe you're on vacation in Italy. Perhaps you're living in a beautiful home with waterfront views. Maybe you've just left your job and won't have to answer another email ever again, at least not a work-related one, anyway.

Feel it and see it, even while staring outside of the window in your studio apartment or sitting at your desk at work. *Know* that change is happening, because it is.

Holding Onto the Past

Every single one of us, at one point or another, has held onto something or someone. Maybe we're holding onto moments we wish never ended. Or, perhaps, we're holding onto moments that negatively affected us, moments we wish never happened at all.

I'm not going to ask you to repress your past or try to forget it in some way. Remember, it's the culmination of your life experiences that's made you who you are today. Your past, whether you look back at it fondly or not, is a part of who you are, and that's ok.

You don't have to forget the things you've been holding onto. Instead allow those memories to pop into your mind, but *don't allow* them to dominate your life, define who you are, or what you're capable of. That's the difference. It's almost like observing those memories from a safer distance. Watching them from afar, for what they were and what they taught you.

You can allow your past to live with you, as a part of who you are, but don't let it hold you back from turning into someone new.

You can redefine who you are every single day if you want to. Your past *does not* define you.
People's opinions of you *don't define you. You* define who you are and what you want to be every single moment, of every single day, week, month and year.
　　The past happened, yes. But, what makes you think that the future can't be better? Why do you feel like you'll never be that happy again? You may have had those same exact thoughts in the past — believing that you'd never be happy again, but then you were.
　　You've held on to moments and have later moved past them. Maybe now you can hardly remember the things that were once so prominent in your mind because you've mentally and emotionally moved so far away from them.
　　How about just going! Going forward. Being your ideal self, living your best life and being truly happy. You don't have to miss out on beautiful memories in the

present because you're instead trying to relive a memory from the past.

Instead, create a new life and fill it with incredible, wonderful, new memories. Look forward to the future while appreciating where you are in the present.

The truth is, you're able to move forward and you can start right now.

Getting Stuck in "Planning Mode"

If you, like so many people, get stuck in "planning mode" you may feel like you're moving closer to your goals when in reality, you aren't making much progress at all.

Maybe you made a plan on how you'll achieve your goals, which is great. But, now, you have to actually follow that plan.

What happens when you start getting close to the end of your plan and the time is rapidly approaching where you're going to need to start making real changes? Do you then decide to change the direction you're going in completely, shifting gears, rewriting your goals and going back to the drawing board? How many times have you already gone through this process? Are you starting to lose count?

I'm sure you have valid excuses for changing course, but get to the root of *why* you keep shifting gears as soon as you start getting close to accomplishing your goals. Why did you *really* shift your focus as soon as you got close to turning your dreams into realities?

If the root cause is fear-based, you're going to have to ascertain what it is that you're truly scared of, and then face those fears. Most of the time, this is a fear-based risk, in the sense that you really do want to complete the goal you set out to achieve, but you make excuses when you get close to achieving it.

You might have imposter syndrome, believing that you aren't actually qualified or deserving of achieving this level of success, so you stop short of your goal and shift gears. There have been countless notable people alive today and throughout history who, I guarantee, didn't believe they were qualified to do the things they did.

If everyone in the world, and throughout history, allowed imposter syndrome to prevent them from moving forward, we never would have progressed as far as we have as a society. Countless incredible inventions may have never come to fruition. Inventors wouldn't have even *begun* the creation process if they believed they either weren't qualified or experienced enough to move forward.

Because people push against their own limiting beliefs, they're able to create new universal truths.

Are you going to tell me you don't think you can do the same? That you're not as smart, talented, or capable as other people who have achieved great things? I don't believe that for a second and I hope by this point, you don't either.

Determine what the real reasons are that have kept you in planning mode. No-one knows what you're thinking — break down your own walls. All you have to do is admit it to yourself and then make positive changes from there.

One way to combat "planning mode" is by ending the cycle. Don't wait another single day before you start making *some* kind of change that will improve your life and help you achieve success beyond the planning phase.

Create mini goals, which are activities you can carry out daily and start today! Make sure the mini goals are actionable right now. You can spend a lifetime intending to do pretty much anything, and you may never really feel prepared or ready.

The more that your actions align with what your goals really are, the more prepared you will feel. There's only one way out and that's through.

That's why it's so important to complete mini goals on a daily basis.

Become as much of a *do-er* as you are a *planner,* and you'll start seeing the fruits of your labor through the positive changes that will begin taking place.

Being a Perfectionist

Perfection truly is the enemy of good, and shockingly, you will get more done and be *closer* to your goals when you stop trying to achieve absolute perfection.

The truth is that your plan is going to evolve over time. Even if you spend months or even years perfecting it, when you actually start putting your plan in motion, things will change.

You will learn new things and as you get more experienced, you will discover more efficient ways of completing tasks as you carry on your journey.

Perfectionism is something I've personally struggled with for years. It was only when I started letting go of the idea of achieving absolute perfection that I started to see real movement in my life. That movement propelled me closer and closer to my goals, which many times exceeded my expectations.

I'm not telling you to accept sub-par results that you're not happy with, not in the least, but start considering if you might see more results by getting the ball rolling and over time, continuing to optimize your approach and strategy in order to hit your goal of absolute perfection. Waiting for perfection can delay, or even halt progress entirely.

It's perfectly fine to have high standards for yourself — it's wonderful in fact and is a quality that many high achieving people have. But when your desire for perfection takes hold to the point where you're becoming stagnant, then you might have a problem on your hands. Ask yourself:

Will I be closer to my goals if I accept nearly perfect results, or should I keep waiting to achieve absolute perfection?

How long might it take to reach my ideal standards?

Is it possible I'll see the most results by starting now, and perfecting later?

In most cases, you can optimize results over time. Therefore, I highly suggest you take the road that brings you the most success, within the shortest time frame, without sacrificing quality or your vision.

You can also redefine perfection. The idea of what the "perfect life" looks like is created by you. Is waiting for perfection just another way of not actually making certain changes in your life? Is it possible that your approach is stemming from a fear of change?

These are the questions you're going to have to honestly ask and answer yourself. The need for everything to be perfect can just be fear in disguise. Push past it. Redefine success if you need to. Whatever it takes to bring you closer to your goals. You can still perfect your goal over time, but get it out there, start making changes, and start living your best life today.

Letting Negative Experiences Define You

Can you think of any challenging experiences you've had that may have only happened once or twice, but since then, you started generalizing who a person is or what a place is like, based on just those one or two challenging moments?

Your reality and your perception of people, places, moments, and events is made in your mind.

Your truth is only true because you believe that it is.

Here's an example: you have an upcoming job interview in a new career field. You've never met anyone in this field, so this will be your first impression of the types of people you'll be working with. You're as excited as you are nervous.

You get to the job interview, looking and feeling your best. You meet the interviewer, they introduce themselves — so far, so good. Your potential future boss sits down, takes one look at your resumé, and then proceeds to go off on you in a way that no one ever has before.

They're shocked at the audacity you had to come in and waste their valuable time with your lack of experience. The interviewer even makes a comment about how poorly put together your resumé is. They ask you, stunned, "What made you *think* you would ever be able to get this job?!"

You stutter, don't know what to say, try your best to hold back the dam of tears from pouring out of your eyes, and then run out of the interview, crying.

After storming off and walking home in the rain (ok, dramatic, but stay with me here,) you start to hate *everyone* in that industry, the industry that you once loved so much. In fact, that was such a traumatic event for you, that you've decided that you no longer want to work in that field at all.

You tell yourself, "If that's how people in this industry are, then I don't want any part of it!" You go back to the old job that you've been trying to quit for the last five years.

Some time passes and your wounded ego is slowly starting to heal, just enough for you to start toying with the idea of working in a new field again. But your last attempt went so horribly wrong that you stop those thoughts dead in their tracks and decide you don't even want to try. You'll do anything to never have an experience like that again, even if it means staying at a job that you hate for the foreseeable future.

Let's file this under, worst-case scenario. The person in the previous example made one attempt to leave their job. They had a very challenging experience while being interviewed and because of that one experience, they decided to stop pursuing a career in that industry entirely. They even chose to stay at the job that they hate, for fear of experiencing another challenging interview again.

Now, what if the person in the example scenario said after the interview:

"Wow, that was a horrible interview, maybe my worst ever! But, I know there's something to be learned from that, admittedly dreadful meeting. If that's how the boss is at that particular job, maybe I don't want to work there. Noted! But, there are still so many other opportunities within the industry. They mentioned my lack of experience as being an issue, as well as my resumé not being put together well.
I'm going to combat both of these grievances by the time I have my following interview. I'll research additional skills or certifications I can receive that pertain to this role and will be sure to redesign my resumé, so it'll be as clear and concise as possible. I'm going to knock the socks off

of the next interviewer and I'll be damned if they don't hire me on the spot!"

Now you're off to your second interview!

People who are successful experience challenges, learn from them, and then apply that knowledge to their future endeavors, increasing their success, knowledge, and resilience in the process.

Even if you had a bad experience, is there anything that you can learn from it? What can you do differently in the future that would help make similar experiences more successful? How did that experience strengthen you and make you more resilient?

Instead of generalizing and never trying again, use those moments as learning experiences and then come back even stronger, more prepared, and more knowledgeable the next time around.

Not Feeling Capable of Succeeding

As I was growing up in a lower-middle-class household, I felt like there was a massive gap between myself and them, them being "successful people."

I used to look at people who were successful as if they were orbiting the rock I was living on. I could see them, but I couldn't touch them, and becoming like them was a dream I didn't even know I was allowed to have.

It took me a long time to learn that there is no them and us.
There is only us and we are all capable of greatness.

I would later come to realize that *me* and *them* only existed in my mind.
Are *they* really more talented than *you* are? No. They're not. In fact, there is no *they* at all!
Other people, *just like you*, did things or placed themselves in situations that increased their chances of succeeding, and then they did succeed.

Now, don't get me wrong, there are a lot of people that have easier times coming up than others. But, even though that exists, it shouldn't deter you from going after your dreams. People who bootstrap their way up to the top have grit and faith in themselves that they can do, literally anything.

You just can't get that if everything is always handed to you. Having that unwavering faith and confidence in yourself is something money can't buy.

Having humble beginnings isn't a bad thing and it definitely isn't something that should differentiate you from anyone else. I encourage you to research the stories of how the people you admire "made it."

Did every single person come from privilege? How many were working regular 9 to 5 jobs before a series of events changed their lives forever? Is money the big separator? That can change in an instant, for anyone, in both directions, losing a lot of money very quickly and also coming into money very quickly. If that's the case, then should money really be what's creating this great divide in your mind?

If talent is what's separating you from other people, let's explore that further. How much of "talent" is really just hard work and practice? Granted, some people can pick things up more quickly than others, but if you were to practice at something every single day, you'd eventually be an expert — bottom line.

So, if talent can be learned, should *that* really be a reason to put other people on pedestals, leaving you looking up? When you come to realize that you're as capable as anyone else, you're placing yourself on the fast track to reaching your goals and achieving success.

Having a Negative Mindset

For some of us, all we have ever known is negativity. Maybe it started in childhood. Being surrounded by friends and family members who lived in fear and felt like most things in life were impossible to attain.

Maybe it's something that we learned as we got older, after attempting to pursue our dreams, but not being immediately successful in those attempts. You might feel like you're incapable of rewiring your thought processes. Almost as if negativity has become so ingrained into who you are that alternative ways of thinking seem impossible to have.

You are the architect of your own reality, and that includes your thought processes and emotional well-being.

You. Not your parents, partners, friends, co-workers, or enemies. There is no benefit to thoughts like, "I won't ever succeed...Nothing good ever happens to me...Everything I try to do I fail at...I'm sure something horrible is waiting for me just around the corner..."

These may be truths to you now, but what you consider to be true, can change. Individual truths are not universal facts. Many are true only because *you* believe they are.

Beliefs like these can just as easily become your new truths: "I am accomplishing my goals every day and will turn my dreams into realities...Good things happen to me all the time...It's crazy how lucky I am...I learn from everything I do and that knowledge is helping me succeed."

You may have negative thoughts pop up without you even thinking about them. It might feel like they're built into your psyche, unalterable. One universal truth is that these thoughts are replaceable, and you have the power to turn those negative thoughts into positive ones.

The first step is to establish where these thoughts are stemming from.

Start working with the most powerful negative thought you find yourself having the most often. Make sure the thought you choose is one that will bring you the most happiness once altered.

Now, there might be some resistance at first, but keep following that rabbit hole. Where does it lead you? What are those memories or feelings that are at the root of this negative thought?

It could be a moment from childhood, an experience you had as a teenager, or an event that happened to you as an adult. Establish the root cause of why you're having this thought.

Repurpose negative thoughts and
turn them into something positive.

Now that you know where these negative thoughts are stemming from, start looking at them from an alternative angle. Ask yourself:

o What am I so scared of, and why?

o Are things really as absolute as I'm making them out to be?

o Is anything really "always" this or that?

o   Am I giving too much weight to one person's thoughts or opinions?

o   Why am I letting one moment define who I am when I already have a lifetime of positive moments that hold more weight?

To rewire your brain and turn a negative into a positive, think about some memories, thoughts or facts that counter that negative thought or moment, proving it untrue.

You know they exist, but this negative thought has been so loud, that you haven't been able to hear anything else. Now it's time to listen.

If, for example, you have a negative thought such as, "I never have a good time when I see my family," you have to ask yourself if that's really 100% true?

Think about some happy memories that you've had with them. Think about times when they were supportive and helpful, when everyone was laughing and enjoying each other's company.

Viewing events through this alternative lens will help you redefine what's true to you. Rarely is anything 100% good or bad. Finding the middle ground will create more balance in your life and can help you look at situations more objectively.

You'll also want to reframe more challenging experiences, as teachable moments you can learn from.

Even if you "fail" at something, and feel terrible about it, think about what you learned from that experience and how that knowledge can help you succeed on your next attempt. Building upon your knowledge in this way will bring you closer to your goal since you're constantly learning from experiences other people may just be classifying as *bad*.

I can't deny the fact that sometimes there are situations that you can't and shouldn't just think positively about. If you're in a bad situation or are being mistreated in some way, I don't want you to just think positively about it. I want you to leave or change that situation immediately. But we can always try to learn something from those moments, either about ourselves or the people around us.

It's important not to be scared of "being negative." You can still have a positive mindset while drawing a line in the sand and declaring that anything crossing that line is unacceptable and won't be tolerated in your life. That can include the way people speak to you or the way you're being treated, either personally or professionally.

Changing a negative mindset into a positive one isn't about making light of a bad situation. The focal point instead is on learning from experiences and seeing them as teachable moments that can assist you on your journey towards your goals and through life.

It's also about moving away from seeing moments and experiences in absolutes, and instead, trying to find the middle ground more often, which will help you have a more well-rounded perspective.

Turning "horrible things that happened," into "teachable moments that aided you on your journey," will change your perspective and will make attaining success more possible.

The following chapter starts by delving into a study that sought to prove that it's possible to change how people feel about negative events that happen to them.

The results are astounding and can help to instill confidence in people's abilities to positively affect their own realities, which can help shape future outcomes. Additional studies on how to manage physical pain, improve stress, and quality of sleep are also analyzed. The steps that participants of the studies took are described at length. Further resources are included at the end of each study as well as at the end of the chapter.

End of Chapter Exercises & Resources

Exercises: Create Your Own *Path to Success*, *Resource Forecast*, and *RAM Table*

- To create your *Path to Success*, first identify each step you need to take to achieve your goal. If one step contains sub-steps, include those as well.
  - ✦ *Use the next page to build your Path to Success.*

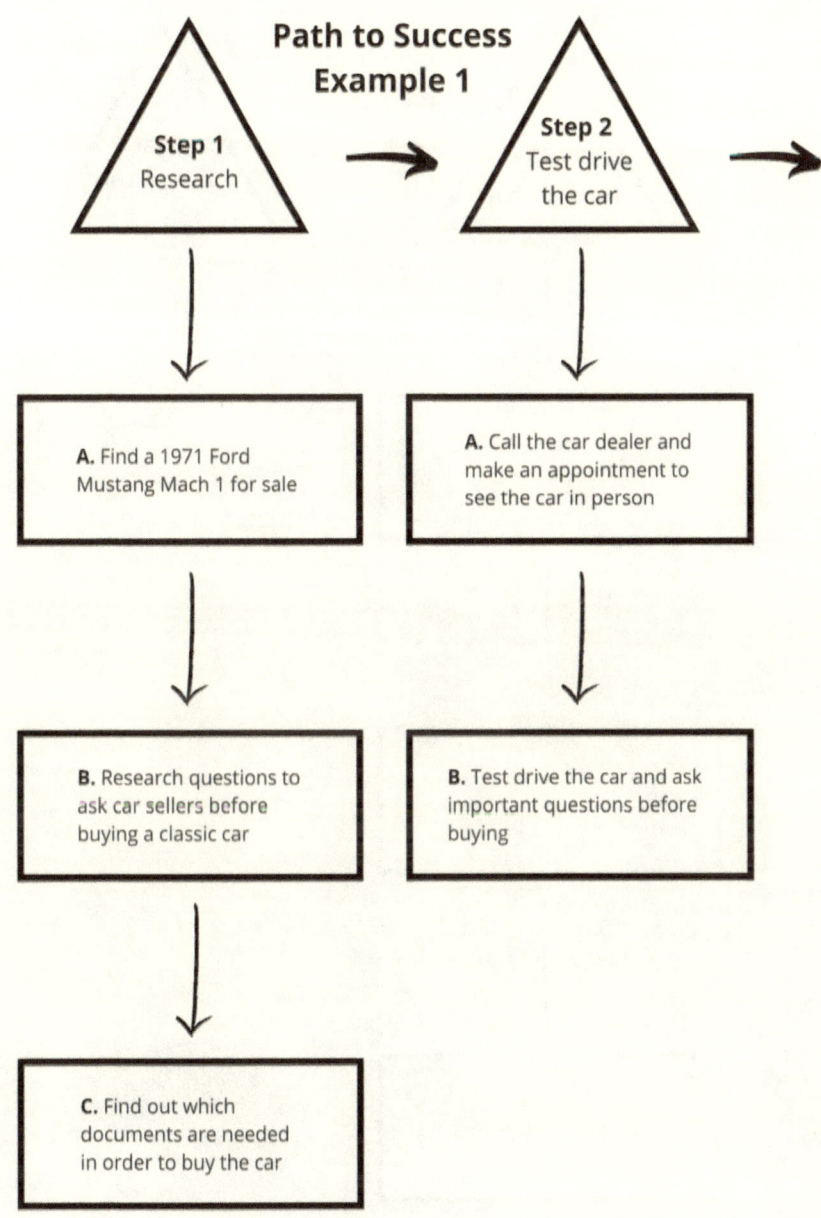

Path to Success
Example 1

Step 1
Research

Step 2
Test drive
the car

A. Find a 1971 Ford
Mustang Mach 1 for sale

A. Call the car dealer and
make an appointment to
see the car in person

B. Research questions to
ask car sellers before
buying a classic car

B. Test drive the car and ask
important questions before
buying

C. Find out which
documents are needed
in order to buy the car

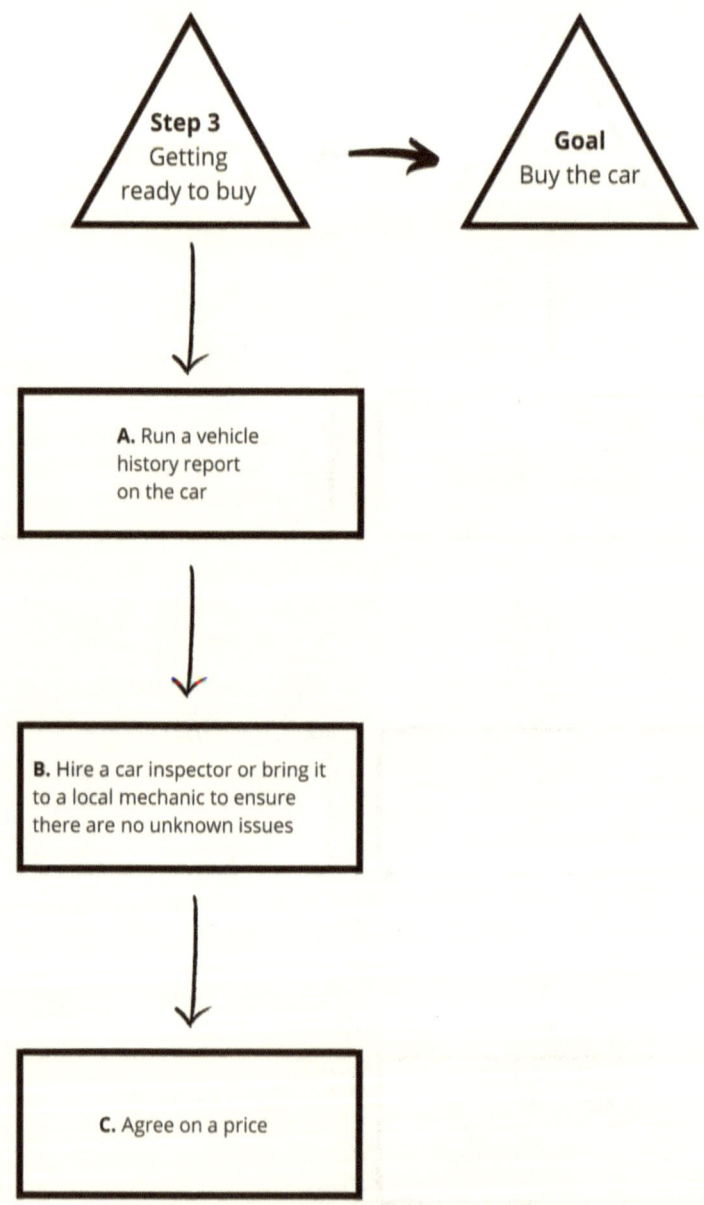

Step 3
Getting
ready to buy

Goal
Buy the car

A. Run a vehicle
history report
on the car

B. Hire a car inspector or bring it
to a local mechanic to ensure
there are no unknown issues

C. Agree on a price

o To create your *Resource Forecast*, list the same steps that you identified while creating your *Path to Success*, and then identify all resources that are required to complete each step.
  ✧ *Use the next page to build your Resource Forecast.*

o As you're creating your *Resource Forecast*, note which resources you have and which ones you'll need.

o Include the steps you'll be taking to acquire all additional resources in your *Resource Forecast*.

Example Resource Forecast

Step on the Path to Success	Resources required to complete each step	Resources I already have	Resources that I don't currently have	Steps to obtaining all required resources
Research	• Time • Computer or smart phone	Computer	Time, in order to conduct research	1. Determine where time is being spent currently 2. Which daily activities can be performed more efficiently 3. Remove all lower-priority tasks to make more time in the day
Test drive the car	Valid drivers license		Valid drivers license	Need to renew expired license
Getting ready to buy	Funds to buy the car	Have $7,500 to spend on car	Need another $7,500	• Move into a higher-paid position • Take on a second role temporarily • Try to work extra hours in my current role and/or get a raise

o While creating your *RAM (Risk Assessment and Mitigation) Table*, you'll be listing the same steps that you identified while creating your *Path to Success*. Establish any potential risks that may arise during each step of your journey.

⟡ *Use the next page to build your RAM (Risk Assessment and Mitigation) Table.*

o After you've established potential risks in your *RAM Table*, give each risk a rating from 1 to 10, stating how severe/damaging the risk would be towards you completing your goal if that risk were to occur. 10 would be the most severe meaning the most disruptive.

o The following section on your *RAM Table* will be the likelihood of the risk happening, which will also receive a 1 to 10 rating. 10 represents a very high or low chance of that risk-taking place.

o The final section on your *RAM Table* is your risk mitigation plan. How will you decrease the chances of risks arising and/or eliminate those risks entirely?

Example RAM (Risk Assessment and Mitigation) Table

Step on the Path to Success	Potential risks	Risk severity	Risk likelihood	How to mitigate risks
Research	My dream car not being available for sale in the city where I live	2	3	If I have to drive further to test drive and pick up the car, that'll be inconvenient, but manageable
Test drive the car	My drivers license is in the process of being renewed. It might not be valid by the time I'm ready to test drive the car	2	5	If needed, my friend can test drive the car for me, as I drive along in the passenger seat
Getting ready to buy	I might not be able to secure funds by the time I'm ready to buy the car	10	2	I almost have all the money needed, but if I'm not able to secure the necessary funds I will try to: 1. Find the same car at a lower cost 2. Do extra freelancing and/or consulting work 3. Watch my spending more closely

Resources

Creating a Path to Success

Miro I Mind mapping software that can assist in the creation of your *Path to Success, Resource Forecast,* and *Risk Assessment and Mitigation (RAM) Table*:

Miro.com

Taking Hold of Your Time

Clockify I Time tracking software.

Clockify.me

Finding Remote Jobs and/or Hiring Employees/Independent Contractors

Indeed & *LinkedIn* I Popular job search engines for posting and searching for jobs.

Indeed.com and Linkedin.com

Behance I The largest online creative network, ideal for finding/promoting talented artists.

Behance.net

Acquiring More Knowledge and Skills

New York Public Library | The *New York Public Library* offers free classes on learning basic computer skills as well as how to code, and use popular software such as *Excel*, *Adobe Photoshop*, *Word*, *PowerPoint*, and more. On-site and remote classes are available.

Nypl.org/events/classes/calendar

Getting Certified

Reddit and *Quora* - If you have questions related to certifications you're interested in receiving, tools to learn, or even what it's like to work in a specific role or industry, you can ask those questions to the users of these two discussion websites.

Reddit.com and Quora.com

Coursera | *Coursera* offers free educational courses online, in addition to paid courses where certifications can be earned. You can receive certifications, and degrees, from world-class universities in fields ranging from computer science and information technology to social sciences, math, and business.

Coursera.org

Google Skillshop I Here, you can take free online courses and receive certifications for *Google* platforms such as *Google Ads, Google Analytics,* and *Google My Business.*

Skillshop.withgoogle.com

Microsoft Certifications I Get certified in *Excel, PowerPoint, Microsoft 365, and more.*

Docs.microsoft.com/en-us/learn/certifications

Books, Ebooks and Audio Books

Amazon I Online retail website offering a wide selection of hardcover, Ebooks, and audiobooks.

Amazon.com

Audible I Online audiobook platform.

Audible.com

Google Audiobooks I Online audiobook platform.

Play.google.com/store/books/category/audiobooks

ThriftBooks I Online bookseller offering an extensive selection of affordable new and used books, including textbooks.

Thriftbooks.com

Online Course Websites

edX | A global nonprofit founded by Harvard and MIT. *EdX* offers free educational courses on a variety of subjects. *EdX* is an excellent resource for continuing education professionally and personally.

Edx.org

LinkedIn Learning | They are a great resource for continuing education, specifically in creative fields, such as photography and graphic design. They also have courses on web development, software development, and business.

Linkedin.com/learning

Udemy | *Udemy* offers courses ranging from photography and IT to productivity, web development, marketing, finance, and academics.

Udemy.com

Starting Your Own Business

U.S. Small Business Administration | A tremendously helpful resource for prospective business owners in America. They offer an abundance of free business resources that can answer many questions that you have about what starting a business entails and how you can do it.

Sba.gov

SCORE | *SCORE* offers remote mentoring for prospective business owners and anyone who has business-related questions.

Score.org

Make a Living off Your Expertise

Squarespace | Affordable website builder for most small business owners.

Squarespace.com

Shopify | Website builder, specifically for e-commerce businesses.

Shopify.com

Etsy | One of the largest online platforms for handmade items.

Etsy.com

Udemy | *Udemy* has really grown in popularity and is one of the most widely used online learning platforms currently. Teachers on *Udemy* offer courses in almost every subject you can think of. From health and fitness to music, finance, personal development, marketing, design and more.

Udemy.com

Skillshare | *Skillshare* is a popular online learning platform that enables users of the platform to teach classes in fields like illustration and music, as well as business, lifestyle, productivity, and web development to name a few.

Skillshare.com

Tracking Your Finances

Mint | *Mint* is a free and an easy-to-use app that's available on both desktop and mobile devices. *Mint* is a budgeting tool created by the makers of *QuickBooks* and *TurboTax*, which allows you to link up all of your financial accounts in one place and then look at your spending and overall finances from a higher level.

Mint.intuit.com

Google Sheets | *Google Sheets* is a free spreadsheet program that offers templates, such as a *Monthly Budget* template. This template allows you to take a more granular look at your finances.

Docs.google.com/spreadsheets

Paving the Way

If you've made it this far, congratulations! Now is the fun part, or at least my favorite part. You've already established what your goal is, you've conducted an ample amount of research while creating your *Path to Success, Resource Forecast* and *RAM Table*. Now it's time to put all that research in motion!

In this chapter, we'll give you the tools to break down barriers that have held you back in the past, paving the way for a brighter future.

Some of those barriers could be physical, such as being in physical pain or not getting adequate sleep. Other barriers could be more internal like negative thought patterns preventing you from being the person you've always wanted to be.

In this section, multiple studies are referenced, and their results analyzed. The studies involve participants overcoming emotional, mental, and physical difficulties. We'll examine how the studies were conducted and explain the steps participants took in order to overcome various challenges in their lives.

Also included are positive affirmations that can help rewire our brains and positively alter thought processes. Affirmations to improve self-image, conquer fear, and improve overall health and well-being are included, as well as guidance on how to create your own.

By having the tools to manage physical pain, improve sleep, increase positive thoughts, and change our inner dialogue, everything becomes possible.

Change Your Thoughts, Change Your Life

The study titled, "Cognitive-behavioural training to change attributional style improves employee well-being, job satisfaction, productivity, and turnover,"[9] was able to prove that attributional styles in employees are directly related to their overall sense of well-being, how satisfied they are with their jobs, how productive they are in their roles, and how likely they were to quit.

Attributional style is the way people interpret events that happen to them. The participants in this study successfully used cognitive-behavioural training to change their attributional styles. The same event can happen to 100 people and each person will *attribute a* different cause to the event. It's about your interpretation of what *caused* the event that changes the way you see it, not the event itself.

If you have a propensity towards interpreting events negatively, the study shows that through cognitive-behavioral training, your mindset can be altered, having significant positive results on emotional and psychological well-being.

---

[9] Proudfoot, Corr, Guest, and Dunn. "Cognitive-behavioural training." 147-153.

Attributional Styles

Positive Attributional Style

For example, let's say someone missed their flight due to an accident on the road. A person that has a more positive attributional style would be left feeling like it *wasn't their fault* for missing that flight. They would instead feel like an unexpected accident on the highway caused the ride to the airport to take longer than usual, which is what caused them to miss their flight.

Alternatively, if a positive event were to happen, like them arriving at the airport early, they would then feel like they made their flight on time because they're punctual and planned ahead.

In this style, the person is *attributing* missing their flight to an external cause that was not their fault (the accident on the highway) meanwhile when a positive event occurs, they *attribute* that event to themselves (arriving to the airport early) and their own capabilities.

Negative Attributional Style

Using the same example, if someone has a negative attributional style, they might *blame themselves* for missing the flight, thinking, "I never should have booked the flight at this time. It's my fault we're late because I chose to fly at this time of day." They might also think, "I always miss flights. Something always seems to happen. Bad things seem to just happen to me."

If something positive were to happen to the person with the more negative attributional style, they would be less likely to *attribute* that positive event to themselves.

If they arrived at the airport early, they might *attribute* arriving early to the driving skills of the person who drove them to the airport, not to themselves in any way.

Differences Between Positive and Negative Attributional Styles

Someone who has a more positive attributional style attributes the causes of good events that happen to them, to themselves. For example, they might feel that a positive event was caused by their own hard work or natural capabilities.

On the flip side, those same people with positive attributional styles will attribute the causes of negative events to external forces that they feel, don't happen very often.

People with more positive attributional styles are less inclined to make blanket statements about how bad things *always* happen to them. Instead, they'll see bad events as *one-offs, events that happen infrequently,* and will usually expect positive outcomes. If a negative event happens to them, they'll then make plans to reduce the chances of that event from happening again in the future.

Someone with a more positive attributional style feels like they have more control over the things that happen to them in life.

If a person has a more negative attributional style, they'll feel like the good things that happen to them are rare and don't happen very often. They feel like they have less control over events in their lives and almost come to expect that negative events will just happen to them, feeling like those outcomes are beyond their control.

How The Study Was Conducted

The study consisted of 166 employees who worked at a British insurance company. Employees were invited to participate in the study, especially if they or their managers felt like the employees were experiencing high levels of stress in their current roles.

The study first established baselines for employee attributional styles, psychological distress, overall job satisfaction, professional self-esteem, and the participants' intention to quit their current roles. Employee sales productivity results were also analyzed.

The program was, "... designed on the CBT manual (Beck, Rush, Shaw, & Emery, 1979) and organizational training principles."[10] Participants engaged in cognitive-behavioural training sessions once a week, every week, for seven weeks. Each session was three hours long.

The sessions included discussions on automatic thoughts, thought recording, goal-setting, time management, task breakdown and activity scheduling.

Study Results

Prior to the study, 71% of participants were experiencing work-related stress and missing sales targets for at least the previous three months. Two-years after the study was conducted, "...65% of the sample achieved sales figures that were above the average or within 5% of the average for their division."[11]

Before the start of the study, only 29% of those participating in the study were actually reaching their sales target.

Three months after the study was conducted:
- Employee turnover decreased by 66%.
- Psychological stress, job satisfaction, and self-esteem all saw major improvements as well.

---

[10] Proudfoot, Corr, Guest, and Dunn. "Cognitive-behavioural training." 147-153.

[11] Proudfoot, Corr, Guest, and Dunn. "Cognitive-behavioural training." 147-153.

The results prove that attributional styles are capable of being transformed, resulting in substantial positive effects on mood, success, and overall well-being.

Actions

The study based its approach on some key cognitive-behavioral therapy principles. To reiterate, sessions with participants included discussions on automatic thoughts, thought recording, goal-setting, time management, task breakdown, and activity scheduling. Let's start by examining these principles.

Automatic Thoughts

Automatic thoughts are the thoughts that emerge in our minds, seemingly beyond our control, and without us making a conscious effort to have them.
Sometimes, we won't even notice they're there. When we do notice their presence, we will either find those thoughts to be helpful or harmful.

If you're about to leave the supermarket and suddenly remember you have to pick something up before going home, that would be a *helpful automatic thought*, since it helped you remember something useful.

However, if you call a friend and they don't pick up, you might automatically think they don't want to talk to you and might not even like you anymore. This would be an example of a *harmful automatic thought*.

How Thought Recording Can Change Automatic Thoughts

By becoming more aware of automatic thoughts, you'll be able to start identifying the events that are triggering those thoughts to occur. Once you establish the events that are tied to those thoughts, start keeping track of:
- The automatic thoughts you're having
- The events that are triggering those thoughts
- Evidence that would prove each automatic thought is true/untrue
- Helpful automatic thoughts to have instead

Through this practice, you'll start catching these thoughts as they arise. This will help rewire your brain, and over time, you'll start having more helpful, positive automatic thoughts.

Goal-Setting, Time Management, Task Breakdown, & Activity Scheduling

Goal-Setting

Setting realistic goals, managing time by identifying time wasters, breaking down large goals into smaller, more manageable tasks, and creating time in your schedule for yourself are just some of the techniques that are used in cognitive behavioral therapy.

When setting goals, make sure your goals are SMART. SMART stands for Specific, Measurable, Achievable, Realistic, and Timely/Time-Bound. A SMART goal states a goal in no uncertain terms.

For example: "I want to spend next September in Italy, followed by two weeks in The Czech Republic and two weeks in Norway, coming back home the first week of November."

This is an *achievable* and *realistic* goal that's also *specific*, *measurable*, and *time-bound*, since it states the countries you'd like to spend time in, the lengths of time you'd like to spend in each country, and when you'd like your trip to begin.

Now that you have a clear-cut goal, make room in your life to complete the tasks that will help you achieve that goal.

Time Management & Activity Scheduling

If you feel like you don't have any time, analyze your schedule and decide which activities you can either remove entirely or perform more efficiently, giving yourself time back in the day to pursue your goals.

It's not uncommon to feel like you're not accomplishing all of your daily goals. Maybe you even feel like you're always putting yourself last, and the things that will make you the happiest always seem to be put on the back burner. Activity scheduling will help to change that.

The first step is to identify the things you'd like to focus your attention on the most. What activities will make you the happiest and bring the most joy to your life?

Do you want to exercise or read more often? Maybe, you'd like to spend more time with friends, or in nature? Perhaps you enjoy painting, sculpting, writing, or taking photographs.

Whatever those activities are, creating time in your day and forcing yourself to participate in them will make you happier and make achieving other goals more likely. Create events/tasks for yourself on your own calendar.

For example, by blocking off an hour a day to work on a project, skill, or even to just decompress, that time is yours and it should not be interrupted. Treat that time as sacredly as you would if that hour was for a work meeting or an appointment with a doctor, client, family member, or friend. It's at least that important. Your happiness is that important.

Task Breakdown

Large goals can feel unattainable but, by breaking them down into smaller tasks, you'll find yourself reaching mini-accomplishments while pursuing your main goal.

This will make the journey to the top more enjoyable, and your large goal will now feel more attainable.

To Learn More

Recommended Reading

Cognitive Therapy of Depression
by Aaron T. Beck, A. John Rush, Brian F. Shaw, and Gary Emery

Mindfulness for Pain Management

The goal of the study, "Mindfulness for Chronic Low Back Pain: A Qualitative Analysis,"[12] was to discover ways of coping with chronic low back pain without the use of medication.

The study explores the experiences of 25 adults, aged 65 and older, as the participants studied mindfulness and meditation in order to treat pain, specifically chronic lower back pain.

Currently, individuals suffering from CLBP, or Chronic Low Back Pain, are most commonly treated with nonsteroidal anti-inflammatory medications, but these drugs can cause adverse side effects and may not be the best course of treatment for everyone.

The techniques in this study can be applied to people suffering from different types of physical pain. By following the same techniques that were used in the study, you might find that you're able to release your physical pain in a way that doesn't rely on medications that could produce adverse effects.

✧ *Always consult your doctor before starting/stopping any medications.*

---

[12] Luiggi-Hernandez, Woo, Hamm, Greco, Weiner, and Morone. "Mindfulness for Chronic Low Back Pain." 2138–2145.

How The Study Was Conducted

Twenty-five adults, all of whom suffered from chronic lower back pain, completed an eight-week mindfulness program and then participated in a focus group after the program ended. All participants were 65 years of age or older.

Since there aren't many documented first-person accounts of people's experiences using mindfulness and meditation to manage pain, this study focuses on the results from individuals' first-hand accounts.

The participants of the study engaged in focus groups where they discussed their experiences in attempting to treat their pain with mindfulness and meditation alone, after having completed the eight-week mindfulness and meditation program.

Study Results

By practicing mindfulness and meditation, participants of the study were able to reduce the severity of their physical pain, which allowed them to become more physically active and increase their quality of life.

Participants spoke about their pain diminishing after practicing mindfulness meditation at varying degrees. The reductions in physical pain varied between participants from no decrease at all to eliminating their chronic back pain entirely. One participant opened up about living with chronic back pain for years, and now for the first time they've released it completely.

Some participants were very fearful of pain at the start of the study, which actually resulted in even *more* physical discomfort. However, by the end of the program, they became less fearful of their pain which assisted in reducing the severity of their pain.

Prior to the start of the study, some participants would try to avoid their pain. Attempting not to think about or focus on their pain, for fear that acknowledging it would amplify their discomfort. But, mindfulness meditation isn't about looking away or denying what's going on with your body or emotions. Instead, it's about becoming aware and more cognizant of who you are and how you feel.

One participant spoke about how it seemed counter-intuitive to *look* at physical discomfort and acknowledge it in order to reduce its severity, yet she found this approach to be shockingly successful. Multiple participants in the study spoke about the importance, significance, and power that they previously gave to their pain.

One individual recalls discussing their pain in casual conversations when asked how they were doing. They would immediately bring up their pain at the start of the conversation. It was that present in their mind, all the time. Now they've taken that power back from their pain, and find themselves rarely bringing it up at all, reducing the significance of their pain in their minds and in their daily lives.

Many participants found that mindfulness meditation made it easier to cope with their chronic pain. It also helped them to reduce the amount of power they gave to their pain and the fear that they had over experiencing it.

Actions

Mindfulness-Based Stress Reduction (MBSR) began in the 1970s at UMass Medical Center in Worcester, Massachusetts by Jon Kabat-Zinn, Ph.D. It was here that mindfulness began to be used to treat chronic pain sufferers.

Today, more and more people are incorporating mindfulness meditation practices into their daily lives with the intention of relieving pain and increasing awareness.

Body scan meditations and mindfulness meditations for physical pain were carried out by participants during the course of the study. While it's best to study MBSR with a certified MBSR instructor over an eight week period, there are ways to learn it on your own as well.

I'll go over some techniques below. Included in the chapter summary are additional resources for learning more about MBSR.

Body Scan Meditation

Body Scan meditation can be carried out in a lying down, sitting, or standing position. It involves bringing gentle awareness to all parts of the body, starting from the feet and moving upward, ending at the top of your head. You'll want to focus on each part of the body, gently, and without judgment.

If you're wearing clothes, how do they feel against your skin? Is there a light breeze in the room that just brushed past your arm or leg, how does that make you feel? It's about bringing awareness to the body as a whole.

Whether you're experiencing enjoyable or painful sensations as you perform body scan meditation, it's important to simply observe these feelings. Try not to react to them, instead just acknowledge their presence and move onto the next part of your body when you feel ready.

Over time, you may start noticing that unpleasant bodily sensations may not seem as severe to you as they once were. The more gentle awareness you bring to your body as a whole, the more you're able to accept sensations as they are, and allow them to pass through you, without needing to react as intensely as you have in the past, before practicing this type of meditation.

Mindfulness Meditation for Physical Pain

You can start this meditation in any position that feels comfortable for you, either lying down or standing up. Once you get situated, find a part of your body that feels either really good or neutral to you at that very moment. You're going to rest your attention here.

Notice what this part of your body feels like. If, as you're focusing on the part of your body that feels good you start to notice an ache or pain, allow your attention to focus on the part of your body that's experiencing discomfort next.

After a few moments, bring your attention back to the part of your body that's feeling good or neutral. Now you're going to switch your focus back again, to the part of your body that's feeling uncomfortable.

So you're essentially shifting your attention back and forth. Moving from the part of your body that feels neutral or good to the part of your body that's in some sort of discomfort.

Now that you've developed a good rhythm, make sure you're still breathing throughout the practice, and start focusing more and more on the neutral/good part of your body, gently shifting your attention away from the part of your body that's uncomfortable.

You're now primarily focused on the part of your body that feels good, but occasionally bring your focus back to the part of your body that's experiencing discomfort.

You're able to experience both of these sensations at the same time. As you are, how does the part of your body that was in discomfort feel now? You'll want to end the session with loving-kindness towards your body and yourself.

To Learn More

Resources to Study MBSR & Mindfulness

UMass Memorial Health Care Center for Mindfulness |
UMass Memorial Health offers 8-week MBSR programs
online.

Ummhealth.org/center-mindfulness

The UC San Diego Center for Mindfulness | UCSD CFM
offers free mindfulness resources online.

Cih.ucsd.edu/mindfulness/mindfulness-compassion-
resources

Guided Meditations

Insight Timer | MBSR Meditations

Insighttimer.com/meditation-
topics/mbsrmindfulness/browse/guided

UCSD Center for Mindfulness | Guided Body Scan
Meditations
Soundcloud.com/ucsdmindfulness/sets/body-scan

Recommended Reading

Full Catastrophe Living (Revised Edition): Using the Wisdom of Your Body and Mind to Face Stress, Pain, and Illness
by Jon Kabat-Zinn

Wherever You Go, There You Are: Mindfulness Meditation in Everyday Life
by Jon Kabat-Zinn

Stress Improvement

The study, "Effect of Transcendental Meditation on Employee Stress, Depression, and Burnout: A Randomized Controlled Study,"[13] sought to determine if Transcendental Meditation could be used to decrease stress and burnout in teachers and support staff members who worked with students with severe behavioral problems at a therapeutic school in Vermont.

What makes TM different from other forms of meditation is the mantra that's used during the meditation sessions which is meant to effortlessly quiet the mind, bringing peace and calm to those who practice. TM is also normally taught by certified TM instructors in one-on-one sessions which is another differentiator from other forms of meditation.

TM (Transcendental Meditation) was popularized by Maharishi Mahesh Yogi. He founded teaching centers, colleges, and schools, making Transcendental Meditation easy to learn and accessible to all.

At the end of this section, you'll find links to some of the establishments that were founded by Maharishi Mahesh Yogi that are still operational today. The effective use of Transcendental Meditation among faculty members opens the door for this form of meditation to be

---

[13] Elder, S. Nidich, Moriarty, and R. Nidich, "Effect of transcendental meditation on employee stress. 19-23.

used by individuals in other high-stress environments, both professionally and personally.

A combination of 40 secondary and supportive staff members participated in the study. The study evaluated staff members' perceived stress levels, feelings of being burnt out, and depressive symptoms before the study began and at the four-month mark.

How The Study Was Conducted

The 40 staffers in the study were placed into two groups. One group would receive a 7-step TM course instructed by two certified TM instructors. The other group acted as the control group, who did not receive TM instruction during the course of the study.

The group that did receive TM instruction was asked to practice TM at home for 15-20 minutes, two times per day, in addition to the TM instruction being led by certified instructors.

Study Results

When comparing the data that was taken at the beginning of the study, to the data received at the four-month mark, the results showed *significant positive outcomes* in the group that participated in the Transcendental Meditation program.

Perceived stress, depression, and overall teacher burnout/emotional exhaustion all decreased in the group practicing TM, with perceived stress improving the most.

The results of the study concluded that staff members were able to effectively reduce psychological stress, depression, and emotional exhaustion using Transcendental Meditation alone.

Actions

It's recommended to study Transcendental Meditation with a certified TM teacher. Below I've referenced reading materials and resources that can be used to find a Transcendental Meditation teacher or meditation center near you.

To Learn More

Study Transcendental Meditation

The Maharishi Foundation USA I A non-profit organization founded by Maharishi Mahesh Yogi.
Tm.org/home-page

Maharishi International University I A non-profit university with on-campus and online degree programs, founded by Maharishi Mahesh Yogi.
Miu.edu

TM I TM Meditation Centers and Teachers Within the U.S.

Tm.org/national-map

TM I TM Meditation Centers and Teachers Around the Globe.

Tm.org/choose-your-country

Recommended Reading

Science of Being and Art of Living
by Maharishi Mahesh Yogi

Improving Sleep

The study, "A Randomized Controlled Trial of Mindfulness Meditation for Chronic Insomnia,"[14] was carried out to determine if mindfulness meditation would be effective at combating chronic insomnia.

The study consisted of 54 participants who were above the age of 21 and met the criteria for insomnia disorder. Some of those factors included difficulty falling and staying asleep.

Participants met the criteria needed to participate in the study if they experienced waking up and staying up for 30 minutes or more for, at minimum, three nights per week for six months or longer.

Some reasons individuals wouldn't qualify to participate in the study were if they were on medications to treat insomnia, had sleep apnea, or weren't proficient in English, since keeping sleep diaries was part of the study.

According to the American Sleep Association, "Insomnia is the most common specific sleep disorder, with short term issues reported by about 30% of adults and chronic insomnia by 10%."[15]

---

[14] Ong, Manber, Segal, Xia, Shapiro, and Wyatt. "Mindfulness meditation for chronic insomnia." 1553–1563.

[15] American Sleep Association. "Sleep Statistics: Data About Sleep Disorders."

Insomnia can be debilitating as it affects mood, energy levels, and even motivation levels.

By finding an effective and safe way to treat insomnia, sufferers are able to feel more energized, get more done, and improve the quality of their lives and their overall health and well-being.

How The Study Was Conducted

Participants in this study were placed into one of three groups:
- Mindfulness-based stress reduction (MBSR)
- Mindfulness-based therapy for insomnia (MBTI)
- Self-monitoring (SM) condition: this group acted as the control group and didn't receive therapy of any kind.

Participants in both the MBSR and MBTI groups engaged in weekly group meetings, for a total of eight weeks. During these meetings, depending on the group they were in, either MBSR or MBTI was taught by qualified instructors.

Individuals in both groups were directed to practice meditation at home six days per week for 30 to 45 minutes per session. Mindfulness-based stress reduction (MBSR) combines different forms of meditation, such as mindfulness, body awareness, walking, body scans and yoga.

Mindfulness-based therapy for insomnia (MBTI) was developed for the purposes of this study.

According to the authors, it's, "...a meditation-based program that integrates behavioral techniques for insomnia." Their goal in developing MBTI was to improve sleep by reducing hyperarousal. This is when the body experiences feelings of extreme panic or anxiety, even when there's nothing happening to be anxious about and no immediate threats are present. A symptom of hyperarousal can be chronic insomnia, since the body starts having an elevated response to stimuli, making sleep very difficult.

Measurements and assessments were taken at the start and end of the study, as well as three and six months after the study concluded. Sleep diaries were kept and monitored throughout the study. Technician-monitored PSG (Polysomnography) sleep tests were conducted at the start, end, and at the 6-month mark of the study.

When the participants were at home, wrist actigraphy devices were used to monitor sleep at the start of the study, when it ended, and again at the 6-month mark.

Study Results

The results of the study found that those who participated in the mindfulness-based stress reduction (MBSR) and the mindfulness-based therapy for insomnia groups (MBTI), *both saw reductions* in the total amount of time that they were awake during the night when compared to the self-monitoring (SM) control group that did not receive any mindfulness training.

However, the mindfulness-based therapy for insomnia group (MBTI) saw the *most* improvement throughout the course of the study, and especially at the 3-month mark, when compared to the mindfulness-based stress reduction (MBSR) group:

"...these findings indicate that interventions featuring mindfulness meditation have positive patient-reported benefits and could be a viable treatment option for chronic insomnia."

Actions

The participants of the study were placed into three groups, with only two groups practicing some form of mindfulness training. I'll expand on how both of the mindfulness-based approaches were carried out below.

Mindfulness-Based Stress Reduction (MBSR)

This group participated in one group meeting every week, for eight weeks. Each meeting was two and a half hours long. Participants also attended a one-time, 6-hour meditation retreat between the 5th and 7th weeks of the study.

"Each group meeting included meditation practice (breathing meditation, body scan meditations, walking meditations, Hatha Yoga), a period of general discussion about the at-home meditation practice, and education on the daily applications of meditation. MBSR was taught by 2 instructors with doctoral degrees (PhD or MD) who had > 2 years of experience teaching MBSR."[16]

Participants were asked to meditate at home at least six days per week for 30 to 45 minutes per session. They were given the book *Full Catastrophe Living* by Kabat-Zinn and a guided meditation CD to use while meditating at home.

Mindfulness-Based Therapy for Insomnia (MBTI)

The MBTI group followed the same instructions as the MBSR group. Both had the same amount of group meetings and additional retreat times. The same meditations took place during the meetings and the same

---

[16] Ong, Manber, Segal, Xia, Shapiro, and Wyatt. "Mindfulness meditation for chronic insomnia." 1553–1563.

at-home meditation instructions were given to participants of each group. The MBTI group received the same book and audio CD as well.

According to the study, the MBTI training differed from the MBSR training in that it included additional strategies for combating insomnia, including sleep restriction therapy and stimulus control.

Sleep Restriction Therapy

You start sleep restriction therapy by keeping a sleep journal for one or two weeks. Some of the things you'd take note of in the journal are:
- The times you get into bed
- The number of times you wake up during the night
- The time of the night you find yourself waking up
- The length of time you're typically awake during those periods

It's also good to include what your diet looked like that day, what time you last ate, if you consumed coffee, tea or alcohol, and whether or not you took drugs of any kind, and if so, when.

Eating within three hours of going to sleep, smoking, drinking alcohol, and using drugs can all interrupt your sleep schedule. Making adjustments to what you consume, and when, can improve your quality of sleep and the length of time you're staying asleep throughout the night.

Keeping a sleep journal establishes a baseline for the actual amount of time you're asleep per night on average. Therefore, it's important to keep track of your sleep as accurately as possible during this time. If after two weeks of keeping a sleep journal, you find out that you're sleeping on average six hours per night, then during weeks three and four, you'll want to establish the same wake-up time for yourself every day, and only spend six hours per night physically in bed.

✧ *Important: You'll want to spend at least five and a half hours in bed every night in order to improve daytime functionality, regardless of how long you're sleeping on average.*

The idea behind sleep restriction therapy is that by establishing how much time you're actually sleeping per night on average, and then only spending that same amount of time in bed for a few weeks, you will be able to rewire your brain to fall asleep more easily and stay asleep longer.

After keeping a sleep journal for one to two weeks (only analyzing your sleep during this time) and spending weeks three and four waking up at the same time every morning, and stepping into bed at the same time every night, you'll start retraining your body to be on a good sleep schedule.

If you find it difficult to get out of bed in the morning, try exposing yourself to as much light as possible and do things that you know will give you a jolt. Open all of the blinds, take a shower, make food, go for a walk, listen to music — do whatever it takes to get up and stay up, especially early on in the process when you'll be the most tired.

You'll most likely be pretty tired for the first couple of weeks of doing this, but that's ok. If you are tired, just make sure you're not operating heavy machinery during that time. You might be tempted to take a nap during the day, but naps will only set you back and won't help you in adjusting your sleep schedule.

By this point you've been keeping a sleep journal for two weeks, followed by two weeks of going to sleep and waking up at the same time. You've also changed your habits to only be in bed for the hours you plan on actually being asleep.

Now, you're in an excellent place to start expanding on the amount of time that you're spending in bed. This will be around week five, where you'll be able to start adding 15-30 minutes to the amount of time you're physically in bed. You don't want to rush the process, so start by adding 15-30 minutes to the amount of time you're spending in bed every week until you reach a number of hours asleep that you feel is sufficient for you.

Stimulus Control Therapy

Stimulus control therapy focuses on reassociating the bed and the bedroom with sleep and sex, exclusively. When you're in bed, you're there to sleep or make love, nothing else.

Start by establishing the same wake-up time every morning. Setting a consistent wake-up time can help regulate sleep and is a significant first step toward getting onto a good sleeping schedule. You'll only enter the bed physically when you're tired enough to go to sleep. So, if you find yourself in bed, tossing and turning and unable to fall asleep, then physically leave the bedroom and do something else.

You may be tempted to cruise the internet on your phone or get some work done on your computer, but these activities will keep you awake longer, so try your best to refrain from using electronics. Instead, read, write or have a chat with a loved one, but don't do these things in the bedroom. Remember, you only want to use the bedroom for lovemaking and sleeping. When you feel yourself getting sleepy, go back into the bedroom, and go to sleep.

It may take a few weeks and you might experience a few sleepless nights, but over time you'll develop better sleep habits, and your sleep will continue to improve.

To Learn More

Resources to Study MBSR & Mindfulness

UMass Memorial Health Care Center for Mindfulness I UMass Memorial Health offers 8-week MBSR programs online.

Ummhealth.org/center-mindfulness

The UC San Diego Center for Mindfulness I UCSD CFM offers free mindfulness resources online.

Cih.ucsd.edu/mindfulness/mindfulness-compassion-resources

Guided Meditations

Breath & Body Scan Meditations from the UCLA Mindful Awareness Research Center:

Uclahealth.org/marc/mindful-meditations

Guided Body Scan Meditations from the UCSD Center for Mindfulness:

Soundcloud.com/ucsdmindfulness/sets/body-scan

MBSR Meditations:

Insighttimer.com/meditation-topics/mbsrmindfulness/browse/guided

Recommended Reading

Full Catastrophe Living (Revised Edition): Using the Wisdom of Your Body and Mind to Face Stress, Pain, and Illness

by Jon Kabat-Zinn

Affirmations

Daily affirmations can help turn your inner voice into a source of strength and encouragement. To start, dedicate a few minutes each day to write down, or say aloud, the affirmations that will be the most impactful for you.

Over time, you won't need to take the time to write them down or even say them aloud. Instead, they will become a part of your subconscious, continually helping you reach your goals and live your ideal life. The following affirmations are meant to get you started and help you gain that unshakeable foundation that you'll need in order to succeed.

Identity

Feeling Confident/Beautiful

✦ When I look in the mirror, I'm proud of who I see and how I look.

✦ It's not about what I wear, but how I feel, and I feel beautiful.

✦ I don't believe I have physical flaws. Instead, there are unique aspects of my body that make me, me, and I'm proud of all of them.

✦ Sometimes I choose to wear makeup to enhance my natural beauty, but I know I don't *need* to wear make-up — no-one does.

✦ I know that what society defines as beautiful is constantly changing, but my confidence in myself will never change. I truly am beautiful inside and out.

✦ I am as beautiful now as I was ___ years ago.

Being Fearless/Brave/Strong

✦ I'm fearless and not scared of, (elevators, heights, auditions, death, etc.) anymore. That's behind me now.

✦ Because I've let go of fear, I'm now able to (take elevators, enjoy hikes on tall mountains, go on auditions with confidence, live my life without being held back by fear, etc.)

✦ I am strong, confident, and capable of overcoming challenges that are presented to me.

✦ I will help others learn how to be strong and brave too, now that I've conquered my own fears.

✦ If I'm scared of something, I *know* I need to face that fear and I will — with bravery and strength.

✦ Being afraid only holds me back. I am finally free and ready to release those fears, moving forward in my new life.

✦ I will take small steps every day to conquer that fear.

Being Successful/Optimistic/Positive

✦ There are many opportunities out there, and I will make sure to put myself in their line of sight!

✦ I know I might encounter difficulties on my path, but I will learn from them and will *not* be deterred because I know that I will be a success.

✦ Negative thoughts will present themselves, but my faith and confidence in myself is strong enough to conquer those thoughts with ease.

✦ When I want to get something done, I get it done. I'm determined to reach my goals and I will succeed, no matter what.

✦ I will create and stick to new habits based on what my short and long-term goals are.

✦ I know I can do anything and I won't allow anyone to tell me otherwise.

✦ Other people have succeeded who are *just* like me. If they did, then so can I.

✦ I've made it this far and I will *not* back down until my goal is fully realized.

Feeling Grateful/Thankful

✦ I've had so much help in my life. I appreciate everyone who gave me a shot, and those who didn't. All those experiences have made me who I am.

✦ I am so thankful to my family, friends, and loved ones for supporting me and being there for me through the years. I will continue showing my gratitude for the contributions they've made to my life.

✦ There are so many people who have made my life more fulfilling (my partner, parents, friends, children). They have shown me so much patience and love when I've needed it the most. I will pass that on to the people whose lives I touch.

✦ I've learned so many lessons from the people around me. Some of those lessons were taught through positive experiences, others through hardships, but I've learned from them all and will continue learning.

✦ I'm so thankful to the people who work tirelessly and selflessly. Healthcare workers, firefighters and first-responders have given their lives to help others, and I will make sure they know how appreciative I am of their service and dedication.

Being Disciplined/Motivated

✦ I'm the kind of person who aims to do 10 push-ups and then does 20. I am in control of my mind and my body and I will not only reach my goals, but I will surpass them.

✦ I am disciplined, confident, and strong-willed. I've created a plan for success and I *will* see it through to its completion.

✦ I am motivated by the people I look up to. These are the people I focus on and aspire to be more like.

Being Strong/Assertive/Direct

✦ I don't allow people to push me around. I *refuse* to be a doormat for others to step on. I am a strong, able-bodied individual and I stand up for myself in positive, constructive ways.

✦ If I disagree with someone or know that something is wrong, I don't second guess myself anymore. I know the truth and I will share it with others confidently and kindly, while being open to their opinions as well.

✦ I am assertive while being calm and kind to others. People respect my approach and I am much more impactful because of it.

✦ I put myself in the shoes of others and encourage other people to do the same, sparking positive change in the world. If I see injustices happening, I speak up.

Being Approachable/Outgoing/Social

✦ My energy is calm and approachable. I make sure my body language is warm and inviting, which encourages new relationships to develop.

✦ I've begun to invite more people into my life, which has allowed me to make more friends and create deeper connections in the process.

✦ I make it a point to call a friend at least once a day and to meet with them at least once a week. This is because I value my friendships and know that my friends appreciate of my reaching out and being present in their lives.

Being Creative/Innovative/Original

✦ I'm not scared to show the world who I truly am anymore. This fearlessness shows in my creative work as well.

✦ I love breaking down barriers and exploring new territories within myself and through different creative mediums.

✦ I'm not scared to make mistakes, I welcome them, and I will continue to learn from them.

Being Mindful & Kind

✦ I am becoming increasingly aware of how my words and actions affect others. By becoming more mindful, I will create positive changes through my words and my actions.

✦ Now, I catch myself when I start reflecting on the past or worrying about the future. I take a breath and that breath brings me back to the present moment.

✦ I'm able to enjoy the present moment for what it is.

✦ I place myself in the shoes of others, even people I once called my enemies. I want to better understand who they are, which will make it easier to understand their points of view.

✦ I support positive change in myself and see forgiveness as a strength.

Being Patient/Balanced/Calm

✦ I used to get angry at little things, now I'm a pillar of strength and patience and don't sweat the small stuff.

✦ I let minor annoyances roll off of me like water off a duck's back. I remain calm even when others become irate. It's through my patience, that patience is taught to others.

✦ I use my breath as a guide for keeping me centered. I take a pause, even when I'm at my angriest, and I come back to the conversation when I am refreshed and able to calmly articulate my thoughts, feelings, and concerns.

✦ I'm in control of my actions. I don't give anyone the power to change my demeanor from being someone who's calm and collected to someone who is loud and rude. I remain centered, even in stressful situations.

New Experiences

✦ I enjoy letting go of control and allowing the world to present new opportunities and moments to me.

✦ I love the unexpected. When plans change I'm flexible and flow with those changes, creating happier moments between myself and the people that I love.

✦ I'm excited to see what the day will bring. I carry positive energy with me everywhere I go and look forward to unplanned moments and experiences.

✦ I love having new experiences and trying new things. I welcome change into my life and want to have more moments that take me out of my comfort zone.

✦ I know that the more experiences I have, the more developed and knowledgeable I will become in a wider variety of topics. I invite these lessons into my life and look forward to them.

Health & Well-Being

✦ I'm not on a diet anymore. Instead, I've changed my mentality towards food and now enjoy eating healthy food that I know will nourish me and make me feel my best. This is the food that I crave most.

✦ I have a healthy relationship with eating. I eat my favorite foods all the time, they just also happen to be good for me.

✦ I'm in control of my body, which is why I eat when I'm hungry, and stop eating when I'm full.

✦ I'm taking charge of my health. I decide what I eat, when I eat, and how much I will eat. My body listens to me, and I want to be happy. Happy to me means being healthy, strong, and feeling my best.

✦ I used to feel like exercising was a chore, now I look forward to taking the time to better myself

✦ I feel a positive connection between my thoughts and my body.

Relationships

Improving Communication/Listening Skills

✦ I used to get angry or leave conversations abruptly. Now, I'm able to communicate how I feel in a calm manner.

✦ I don't just wait to speak while in a conversation. Instead, I'm actively listening to the person who's speaking. I want to get to know them better and be present for them on a deeper level.

✦ I've learned how to read my partner's body language. So I know when they are really asking for love and when it's best to give them space

✦ I choose my words more carefully when in arguments.

✦ During fights, I know that my partner is in as much pain as I'm in, which is why I want my words to heal their wounds, not create new ones.

Increasing Trust

✦ Instead of resorting to anger, I communicate to my loved ones the reasons for my distrust. Through this open dialogue, we're able to connect with each other on a deeper level and build trust and mutual respect.

✦ In the moments when I find myself not trusting others, I try to find evidence that either confirms or denies these thoughts. Oftentimes, my distrust is fear-based and there's no evidence to back it up which turns distrust into trust.

✦ I trust that my loved ones want me to be happy and will do everything in their power to honor that trust. They have demonstrated this time and time again across the ___ months/years that I've known them.

✦ There are moments when fear and distrust may arise. Instead of allowing myself to spiral, I get to the root cause of those fears and my own distrust. By analyzing the source, I'm able to realign my thoughts and effectively combat those negative feelings.

Making More Time/Being More Romantic

✦ I make time for my partner every day. They're always so available to me, I want to be as available to them.

✦ I will date my partner again, reigniting that spark that we had when we first met. By spending quality time with one another and creating romantic situations, our love for each other will grow, and the relationship will continue to flourish.

✦ I will do something nice for my partner every single day. Whether that's a massage, drawing a bath, or cooking a romantic meal. Every day I will make an effort to show them how much I genuinely care.

Letting Go of the Past in Relationships

✦　　While in a heated conversation with my partner, I don't bring up moments from the past. Those are wounds that are trying to heal and continuously opening them up will not aid in the healing process. So instead, I stay in the present moment and only discuss current issues and how to resolve them.

✦ I forgive myself for mistakes that I have made. I learn from my mistakes and make sure that they aren't repeated. I forgive my partner for the mistakes they've made as well and leave them out of present conversations in order to move on from them and allow change to take place.

✦ I've let go of painful memories and have learned how to forgive my partner for them. This forgiveness has allowed us to truly move on from the past, enjoy the present, and look forward to our future.

End of Chapter Exercises & Resources

Exercises: Creating Your Own Affirmations

o Create a list of daily affirmations, speaking about your goals in the present tense.
  ✧ *Review your answers from the Gaining Clarity chapter to help you write affirmations that correspond to your goals.*

_____

_____

_____

o What time of day will you recite your affirmations (either silently or out loud)?
  ✧ *Set a time of day for saying the affirmations you created either internally or out loud.*
  ✧ *It's best to start and end the day with affirmations. If it will help you can link up your affirmation time with another activity. For example,*

maybe each day while your coffee is brewing you will take a few moments to work on your affirmations.

_____

_____

_____

Resources

Change Your Thoughts, Change Your Life

Recommended Reading

Cognitive Therapy of Depression
by Aaron T. Beck, A. John Rush, Brian F. Shaw, and
Gary Emery

Mindfulness for Pain Management

Resources to Study MBSR & Mindfulness Meditation

UMass Memorial Health Care Center for Mindfulness I
UMass Memorial Health offers 8-week MBSR programs
online.

Ummhealth.org/center-mindfulness

The UC San Diego Center for Mindfulness I UCSD CFM
offers free mindfulness resources online.

Cih.ucsd.edu/mindfulness/mindfulness-compassion-
resources

Guided Meditations

Insight Timer I MBSR Meditations

Insighttimer.com/meditation-
topics/mbsrmindfulness/browse/guided

UCSD Center for Mindfulness I Guided Body Scan
Meditations
Soundcloud.com/ucsdmindfulness/sets/body-scan

Recommended Reading

*Full Catastrophe Living (Revised Edition): Using the
Wisdom of Your Body and Mind to Face Stress, Pain,
and Illness*
by Jon Kabat-Zinn

*Wherever You Go, There You Are: Mindfulness
Meditation in Everyday Life*
by Jon Kabat-Zinn

Stress Improvement

Study Transcendental Meditation

The Maharishi Foundation USA I A non-profit
organization founded by Maharishi Mahesh Yogi.
Tm.org/home-page

Maharishi International University I A non-profit university with on-campus and online degree programs, founded by Maharishi Mahesh Yogi.

Miu.edu

TM I TM Meditation Centers and Teachers Within the U.S.

Tm.org/national-map

TM I TM Meditation Centers and Teachers Around the Globe.

Tm.org/choose-your-country

Recommended Reading

Science of Being and Art of Living
by Maharishi Mahesh Yogi

Improving Sleep

Resources to Study MBSR & Mindfulness

UMass Memorial Health Care Center for Mindfulness I UMass Memorial Health offers 8-week MBSR programs online.

Ummhealth.org/center-mindfulness

The UC San Diego Center for Mindfulness I UCSD CFM offers free mindfulness resources online.

Cih.ucsd.edu/mindfulness/mindfulness-compassion-resources

Guided Meditations

UCLA Mindful Awareness Research Center I Breath & Body Scan Meditations.

Uclahealth.org/marc/mindful-meditations

UCSD Center for Mindfulness I Guided Body Scan Meditations.

Soundcloud.com/ucsdmindfulness/sets/body-scan

Insight Timer I MBSR Meditations

Insighttimer.com/meditation-topics/mbsrmindfulness/browse/guided

Recommended Reading

Full Catastrophe Living (Revised Edition): Using the Wisdom of Your Body and Mind to Face Stress, Pain, and Illness

by Jon Kabat-Zinn

Success from Humble Beginnings

The path to success looks different for everyone. Some people become successful very quickly, while for others it can take weeks, months, or even years before they reach their goals. One thing that is true for everyone is that there are a series of steps that are taken and moments that are experienced before a goal is accomplished.

Without every single one of them, you could not accomplish your goals. Those include the moments when you're on top of the world and those that are significantly more challenging.

Believing that success is possible might be the biggest challenge you'll need to overcome in order to succeed.

I know, I know, but how can that be one of the biggest challenges? There are undoubtedly obstacles that will need to be conquered, but in my experience, many people don't even *try* to reach specific goals because they don't believe those goals are possible to achieve.

This means, sadly, that they've cut themselves off from learning how they might be able to succeed since they never tried in the first place. Their dreams died before they ever started exploring ways of achieving them, because they didn't believe their goals were possible to attain.

If you've tried and failed a dozen times, you've gained knowledge and experience through those attempts. Even with 100 "failures" you're still 10 times closer to success than someone who has never been brave enough to try at all.

By changing this thought pattern and building the staircase to your dreams, you can turn these thoughts around and success can be within reach once again. Experiences and events build on top of each other and success is no different.

I'm sure you've listened to people as they've discussed how they got to where they are in their careers and in their lives. These stories often sound something like this, "I was nowhere, and then this happened. Because that happened, this next event occurred. As that was going on, I met so-and-so and then—boom! Overnight I became a success!"

Now, that may be a success story, but it certainly didn't happen overnight. Don't get me wrong, there are people who achieve success more quickly than others, but every person's journey consists of a series of events. It's the culmination of those events that lead each individual to their destination.

Even the "overnight success stories" still had a chain of actions and reactions that brought them to a place in life that allowed them to succeed.
The absolute worst thing that can happen if you attempt to achieve your dreams is that you "fail." I hesitate to even use that word, but ok, you "fail," but you learn

something. You either learned what not to do or how to do something in a better way.

Failure only exists when you stop trying.

The education aspect is very important because, without it, you could just keep carrying out the same attempts over and over again without achieving your desired results. By analyzing why certain initiatives are working and why others aren't, you're building the road that will take you to your destination instead of just going in circles.

Sometimes we receive education in very difficult, soul-crushing ways. I remember entering new fields throughout my life and having crippling anxiety each time. I was even physically ill during some especially difficult times, but even during those periods I knew that I was on the right path and that I was learning every single day, however painful the process may have been.

Perhaps, it was the hard way, but it was a path on the journey to success and I'd rather be on that path in total anguish than living day-to-day *not* pursuing my goals and instead just accepting my lot in life.

As I speak about the difficulties you may face on your journey, don't let those difficulties scare or deter you in any way. Mentioning the challenges you might face is meant to prepare you for the road ahead so you're better equipped to handle them if they arise.

Now, when you do face potential roadblocks, for one, they won't surprise you, and two, they won't slow you down in the least since they're likely just natural occurrences on your journey.

I'm going to give you some advice I wish someone would have told me when I first started pursuing my goals:

You have to accept the fact that as you try new things/learn new skills, you will be really bad at first, horrible even!

But over time, you'll keep learning and keep improving. This is the road to eventually becoming an expert.

If you want expert status, you have to go through the sucking part first, especially if your goal requires new skill sets that you haven't acquired yet. The way to get around this potentially demoralizing and humiliating learning curve is by not expecting too much from yourself at first. Do your best and work hard of course, but don't expect that you will be even remotely good for some time.

Instead, take solace in the fact that you are learning and as you continue practicing, success will no longer just a possibility, but an inevitability!

If someone would have told me these things when I first started, I'm sure my crippling anxiety wouldn't have been nearly as crippling.

To their credit, the person who did give me that advice was my partner who has stuck with me during the best of times and the worst of times. He too followed a similar path and it was only once we were both years into our new career fields that these revelations were made — better late than never!

We all want to do a good job and it's very common for there to be a certain level of nerves present when you want to succeed. Being able to let go of the extra anxiousness however, is much healthier and ironically, you'll probably perform better without the unnecessary added stress.

The sense of accomplishment of just being in pursuit of a life-altering goal makes falling down and picking yourself back up again worth it. I guarantee you will be learning more about life following your dreams than if you were never to try at all.

Do you want a life where days just blend together, and there isn't much to look forward to?

Personally, I'm excited to place myself in situations that challenge me and are actively bringing me closer to my goals. It's these experiences that turn us into the ideal versions of ourselves, the versions that we've always wanted to be. There are millions, if not billions of people out there who want to know how to change their lives in some way. I believe that if they knew how, and more importantly, if they believed they could, they would.

I've had 22 different jobs across 10 unrelated fields in 16 years of being in the workforce. Those fields include the entertainment industry, service industry, real estate, teaching English as a foreign language, sales/marketing, project management, and team leadership. The amount of knowledge that I've gained from taking the road less traveled is unprecedented. For me, the goals that I've had in life have been primarily based around creative and travel-related pursuits.

Working in the service industry allowed me to have a great deal of flexibility in my life, but eventually, my goals changed, and the service industry wasn't supportive of those goals anymore. That's when I knew I had to make a change.

I had spent nearly 10 years in the service industry, mostly bartending, but I've done it all. Host, bar back, server, runner—everything. I had no skills outside of bartending and I had no idea how I would leave an industry I've been in for the better part of a decade. I didn't know what I would do, but I knew what my goal was.

My goal was to leave the service industry and start making a living in a career field that would allow me to develop new skills in the areas I was most interested in.

At the time, those areas were photography and photo editing.

I didn't feel prepared to enter this new field, but eventually, I got over that feeling, created a resumé, and started applying for jobs. A lot of them.

Eventually, someone actually wanted to set up an interview with me! I was stunned and already sick to my stomach. But I went anyway, and even more shockingly, I got the job.

It paid less than my bartending position, but I knew I'd be able to get higher paid roles over time and at least match what I was making behind the bar. It was my first 9 to 5 office job, ever. Office life had always intimidated me, but with my goal of leaving the service industry, I knew I had to at least try it out.

I managed to convince these people to hire me for a job I couldn't have been more underqualified to do. I tried my best and spent all of my down time studying for the role in addition to the work I was putting in at the office.

Each day was torturous and I never felt more like a failure in all my life, but wow did I learn a lot.

I was primarily retouching photos in this role. I loved photography and figured I'd try to make a living in ways that related to photography. Photo retouching is part of that field so, to me, it made sense to move in that direction.

I was awful at it, but I really did try. I would go home and practice using the same software that I was using at the office. I watched tutorial after tutorial, but still, when I'd sit back at my desk every morning, I'd feel nothing but panic and dread. Whatever knowledge I had acquired the night before seemed to have disappeared into thin air. I was that nervous. There have been only a few times in my life where I was that on edge, but hey, we all have to start somewhere!

I eventually left that job and started freelancing as a photographer and as a photo retoucher, which gave me twice as many job opportunities. I studied tools like *Adobe Photoshop* extensively and eventually got pretty good.

I also took online photography courses and practiced taking photos in my off time. I created an online portfolio for myself and now that I had that one job under my belt, I figured others would follow, and others did. I continued freelancing for about a year before my partner and I eventually decided to move to Los Angeles.

That's where I got a retouching job at a major home furnishing distributor. I felt like all my hard work was finally paying off! At the time, this was the best-paid position I had ever had, and it was one where I was surrounded by creative and talented individuals that I learned a lot from.

Within a few months of working in this role, I was editing photos that were circulating on the covers of magazines being sent out to households across the country. This is with less than two years of experience retouching photos.

I stayed in this position for some time, but eventually, I started considering what working remotely would be like. I wanted more time to work on personal projects, and since there's no commute when working from home, I would have at least an extra 2-3 hours each day being in a remote position.

By this time, I had gotten pretty good at photo-editing, and *it is* a career that could be done remotely. Was there a large demand for that kind of work, and could I get a remote job editing photos?
I didn't know, but what I did know was that I had to keep searching for a role that would give me the level of flexibility I was searching for, and eventually, I found it.

I worked one more on-site job after leaving my photo-editing position, but this job offered one remote day per week. This was the closest I'd ever come to working remotely, and I was happy to accept the role.

I reached my original goal of leaving the service industry, but I still wasn't in a 100% ideal position. I think it's important to remain appreciative and grateful for what you have in the moment, but you can still strive for more, and strive for more I did. There's a healthy balance that needs to be struck between wanting more and being happy where you are, but I definitely think it's possible to achieve.

My new goal was to make a living working 100% remotely and to travel the world, seeing as many places as I can while consistently earning a living doing something I enjoyed.

I started by performing *Google* searches around, "how to make a living working remotely," and I started considering which roles I could possibly take on. At that time, I considered alternative paths I could go down. I was looking into certifications I could receive and tools I could familiarize myself with that could be added to my resumé.

I found some websites that allow you to look for remote work and so, I started applying. And again, I was shocked when I actually started landing roles. But, I was doing it! I was making a living working from home.

Now, it wasn't a great living, not at first, but it was something, and more importantly, it was proof that it was possible, and for me, breaking past that barrier of entry was the most challenging part of the process. I was working remotely editing photos, doing data entry, anything I could possibly do, I did.

Over time I became less and less surprised when I would get work, but it did take living this life for a good 2-3 years before I started to believe it really was *my* life. It sounds weird, but when you're used to living a certain way and then everything about your life changes, it's shocking, and to me, I just kept waiting for the other shoe to drop.

At one point, I wasn't sure if I could make a living outside of the service industry. I felt like I had no skills and nothing to offer an employer in any other field, so why would anyone want to hire me? Then, the more work I started to get and the more skills I acquired, the more real it became.

I felt the same exact way about working remotely. I knew some people who did it, but it seemed so unattainable to me, but I had to try. Eventually, I was able to make a living working 100% from home.

Each time that I've gone through this process of doubting what's possible, trying to achieve it, and then succeeding, my faith in what can be done and what I can do, grew.

I've learned that if I make my goal specific, do the research on how to accomplish that goal, and then start making arrangements in my life that make room for my goal to exist, that I will succeed and I will eventually be living that ideal life.

I accomplished my goal of working remotely in a field I enjoyed working in. With the accomplishment of a goal, a new one is born in its place. My next goal was to improve my finances.

Within two years of working 100% remotely, I was able to triple my income, following the exact path that I outlined in *Motion*. I did this by taking on multiple low-demanding, remote roles that I knew I could handle and would thrive in before eventually moving into one higher-paid permanent position.

Without a daily commute, I had over three extra hours per day, which made any additional work that I'd take on feel much more manageable.

Working in an on-site position, you can't take on multiple roles, unless you're working nights and weekends which to me aren't options. I have a life to live and I'm not about to give all my time to a job. I prefer spending time on myself, with my friends, family, and loved ones.

By taking on these multiple roles, I wasn't just making six figures. I was paying off debt that I've been trying to pay down for nearly 10 years. I was able to provide for my parents and do nice things for my friends and other family members. My entire quality of life changed and as my life improved, people's lives around me improved as well.

But remember, if you are going to double up on work, put a cap on the amount of time that you stay in multiple roles. I used the extra income as a stepping stone to reach other goals. With the right planning, this could be a good strategy to move on to your next goal and into the next phase of your life. Now, for a familiar story. After I left the service industry I got a job in a photo-editing position. That taught me the skills I needed to get other jobs and eventually work remotely. Because I was working remotely, I was able to live and work out of major U.S. cities while traveling and earning an income the entire time. Seemingly overnight, my income tripled, all while working remotely.

Working remotely might not be a goal for everyone, but I encourage you to consider if this life would be more suitable for you and if it could help you reach other goals more quickly. It certainly helped me.

It gave me more time, since I didn't have a commute to worry about. In New York City and in Los Angeles where my average commutes have been about an hour and a half each way, having three extra hours each day gave me the ability to take on additional work, but it also improved other areas of my life as well.

I took care of my health more, was able to prepare better food for myself at home, to spend more time with my partner, and to keep in touch with family and friends more since I was more relaxed and had more free time on my hands. I even got to do more cleaning and was able to spend more time with my pet.

I was able to pursue larger goals with the extra time I had, such as playing guitar, learning how to cook, studying Italian, traveling more, going to more art and music shows, and even watching more movies — which I love!

This is my success story and remember, there are many ways to define success, but the only definition of success is what success means to you.

The following stories are of real people who succeed in ways that most wouldn't have ever imagined. They didn't grow up in environments that made success easy to attain, yet here they are. Living proof that you can succeed: all you have to do is try.

Entrepreneur | Oprah Winfrey

"I truly believe that thoughts are the greatest vehicle to change, power, and success in the world. Everything begins with thoughts."
Oprah Winfrey[17]

We all know who Oprah Winfrey is. You might know her from her successful T.V. show *The Oprah Winfrey Show*, from her book club, from one of the six books she's written or maybe you subscribed to her magazine *O, The Oprah Magazine*.

She's made countless movie appearances, runs her own T.V. network, *The Oprah Winfrey Network (OWN)*, and even had an exhibition at the Smithsonian's National Museum of African American History and Culture called "Watching Oprah: *The Oprah Winfrey Show* and American Culture."

She has donated millions of dollars to numerous charities throughout her career and started The Oprah Winfrey Leadership Academy for Girls in South Africa. In fact, she's one of the most influential and inspirational people of our time, and I'm not the only one who thinks so.

---

[17] "Young Oprah Winfrey interview on her Life and Career." 7:50. YouTube.

Oprah Has Received a Multitude of Awards and Honors

Oprah Winfrey was named by *Time Magazine* as being one of the top 100 people "...who most affect our world."[18] in 2010.

USA Today included Oprah as one of the "Women of the Century for arts, literature and media," in 2020.[19]

Oprah has been recognized by multiple publications, including *Forbes*, as being one of the wealthiest self-made women in America.[20]

Oprah has also built a reputation as being one of the most generous women in America. In 2004 she was recognized by *Businessweek* as being the first African American to make the Top 50 Philanthropist List.[21]

The Presidential Medal of Freedom was awarded to her by President Barack Obama in 2013.[22]

She received The Cecil B. DeMille Award for lifetime achievement at the 2018 Golden Globes.[23] She was also the recipient of The Jean Hersholt Humanitarian Award in 2011.[24] "The Jean Hersholt Humanitarian Award, an Oscar statuette, is given to an "individual in

---

[18] Donahue. "Oprah Winfrey - The 2010 TIME 100." TIME.com.

[19] Schnell. " Oprah on USA TODAY list." USA Today.

[20] Dolan and Wang. "America's Richest Self-Made Women 2021." Forbes.

[21] "Online Extra: A Talk with Oprah Winfrey." Bloomberg.com.

[22] "Obama Awards Presidential Medal of Freedom." 41:35. YouTube.

[23] "Oprah Winfrey's Golden Globes speech" CNN.

[24] "Oprah to receive humanitarian award." CBS News.

the motion picture industry whose humanitarian efforts have brought credit to the industry.'"[25]
"Oprah Winfrey was inducted into the Television Academy Hall of Fame in 1994."[26] She was the *first* recipient of the Bob Hope Humanitarian Award in 2002.[27] She was even inducted into the National Women's Hall of Fame in 1994.[28]

Humble Beginnings

Oprah Winfrey was born at home in Kosciusko, Mississippi on January 29, 1954. Her birth name is Orpah Gail Winfrey. Orpah was chosen as it's a biblical name, but since people had trouble pronouncing it, the "p," and the "r," became switched, and over time the name Oprah came to be.

For the first six years of her life she was raised by her grandmother, Hattie. Oprah's mom, Vernita, gave birth as a teenager and out of wedlock, which is why her grandmother stepped in to help. Vernita moved North to Milwaukee shortly after Oprah was born in the hopes of pursuing a better life for both herself and her daughter.

---

[25] "Jean Hersholt Humanitarian Award." Oscars.org

[26] "Oprah Winfrey - Emmy Awards." Television Academy.

[27] "Oprah Winfrey accepts the Bob Hope Humanitarian Award." Television Academy.

[28] "Oprah Winfrey Hall of Fame Induction 1994." Television Academy.

Oprah believes that being raised by her grandmother truly saved her life. Her grandmother taught her to read and this, Oprah felt, gave her the "...foundation for success,"[29] that she needed. She doesn't believe the same educational opportunities would have been available to her had she moved to the North with her mother, as Vernita's life during this time was less stable.

"Somewhere I've always known that I was born for greatness in my life. Somewhere I've always felt it. I remember being on my grandmother's farm and knowing at four years old. I just always knew"
Oprah Winfrey[30]

Oprah loved her grandmother and didn't really know her mother very well as a child, having spent the majority of her life being raised by Hattie. She knew her mother as her mother, but didn't feel that same level of comfort or the same connection that she did with her grandmother.

When Oprah was six years old, she joined her mother up North, but no one ever explained to Oprah what the reasons were behind the move. So naturally, this made the move especially difficult for her. Now

[29] "Young Oprah Winfrey interview on her Life and Career." 14:20. YouTube.
[30] "Oprah Winfrey 1988 Barbara Walters Interview." 10:21. YouTube.

Oprah was being taken away from her grandmother and raised by her mother, who she hardly knew.

Vernita was working as a housemaid and lived in a house with another woman. Oprah recalls not being allowed to sleep inside the house on her first night of living with her mother. Upon meeting the owner of the house, Oprah describes knowing instantly that she was looked at unfavorably because of the color of her skin. She believes this is why she wasn't allowed to sleep in the house that first night and instead slept on the front porch area.

Although this was a particularly challenging time for Oprah, she remained studious and used books as an outlet to other worlds. After learning how to read, she would read books written primarily by female authors. These have always been of great inspiration to her and taught her as a young girl living in poverty, that there were other ways of living.

Oprah has spent the majority of her life speaking in front of large groups of people. The first speech she ever made was in her hometown of Kosciusko, Mississippi when she was three and a half years old.

She made an Easter speech at a Baptist church and remembers even then; the church attendees being impressed by her speaking abilities.

Oprah went through some rebellious years in her youth, which lasted until the age of 14 when she was sent to live with her father, which she describes as being her salvation. Her father was strict and told her at a young age that she was an A student and A students don't bring Cs into the house, and so she didn't. From that moment on she studied hard and brought those A's home.

She worked hard at her studies and at the age of 17, got her first big break in broadcasting.

Oprah was chosen along with one other student in the state for a White House Conference on Youth, and so she was interviewed by a local radio station.
A year later at the age of 17, the same person who interviewed her, remembered Oprah and asked her to represent the radio station during the Miss Fire Prevention Contest. She entered and as the only woman of color in the contest, she felt very relaxed because she didn't believe she had a shot at winning.

When the time came for the participants to answer a question on what they would do if they had a million dollars, the other participants gave the typical answers you might expect. They said they'd give the money to the poor or buy their dad a truck, but when it was Oprah's time to answer she said, "...if I had a million dollars, I would be a spending fool. I'm not quite sure what I would spend it on, but I would spend, spend, spend."[31]

Another question in the contest that Oprah answered was what she'd like to do with her life.

---

[31] "Young Oprah Winfrey interview on her Life and Career." 31:30. YouTube.

To this, she didn't really have an answer, but she remembered seeing Barbara Walters on T.V. that morning and since Barbara was a woman who Oprah admired, she said that she, "...believed in the truth and was interested in proclaiming the truth to the world."[32] Oprah won the contest.

"I look back on my life and I think, when you ask me about how did I get to be here, there are so many little pieces to the process that has helped me to be who I am."
Oprah Winfrey[33]

After winning the contest, she went back to the radio station where she was asked if she'd like to hear her voice on tape, just as a fun thing to do after the contest.

She did and before she knew it, she was hired on the spot by the radio station. She was still in high school at this point, so she would go to school during the day and after school, she was doing on-air newscasts.

A few years later, now a sophomore in college, someone reached out to her and said, "We heard you on the radio, would you be interested in working in television?"[34] Oprah rejected this offer on *three separate*

---

[32] "Young Oprah Winfrey interview on her Life and Career." 32:03. YouTube.
[33] "Oprah Winfrey 1988 Barbara Walters Interview." 19:10. YouTube.
[34] "Young Oprah Winfrey interview on her Life and Career." 33:08. YouTube.

occasions since she felt like accepting it would mean she wouldn't finish college.

It wasn't until a college professor told Oprah, "...don't you know that's why people go to school, so that somebody can keep calling them?"[35] Referring to the opportunity that was being presented to her through the job offer she kept rejecting. That resonated with her and so she accepted the offer and went to an interview at the station.

"I don't believe in luck. I think
luck is preparation meeting opportunity."
Oprah Winfrey[36]

During the interview with the news director, Oprah, being 19 and not having any experience working in television, didn't really know what to do or how to act in order to get the job. But, she loved Barbara Walters and since Barbara was a successful woman in journalism, Oprah decided to emulate her mannerisms.

From how Barbara's legs were positioned to more obvious gestures, such as looking up, down, and then up again during interviews. Oprah carefully studied and successfully emulated Barbara's body language. Needless to say, she got the job.

---

35 "Young Oprah Winfrey interview on her Life and Career." 33:25. YouTube.
36 "Young Oprah Winfrey interview on her Life and Career." 04:06. YouTube.

Extraordinarily enough, years later Oprah would end up being interviewed by the very woman she looked up to, Barbara Walters.

"Be willing to admit that you know nothing."[37]
"You don't have to be perfect."[38]
Oprah Winfrey

Oprah knew she just needed to get her foot in the door which is why when she was asked by the news director about her background, she made it seem like she was much more experienced than she really was.

When asked if she knew how to edit, she said yes. When asked if she knew how to report on stories, she said yes. The truth was, that she had no experience at all and really was tremendously underqualified for the job, but she didn't let this stand in her way.

She knew that she was a hard worker and once shown how to do something, she would be able to do it. She had faith in herself and in her abilities, but that doesn't mean she didn't need a little help to get started.

She walked into her first day on the job at a city council meeting and announced to everyone there that she had no experience and she needed help. Help was provided to her by the people she was surrounded by and this became the start of her television career.

---

[37] "Young Oprah Winfrey interview on her Life and Career." 47:08. YouTube.
[38] "Young Oprah Winfrey interview on her Life and Career." 02:57. YouTube.

Oprah, being an avid reader, loved the book *The Color Purple*, by Alice Walker. When she read the first page, she wept. It touched her so deeply and resonated with her on a higher level. She remembers reading it and being so obsessed with the book and how impactful it was for her, that she bought multiple copies and gave them to people that she knew, even to total strangers!

When she found out that there was a movie coming out based on *The Color Purple*, she told everyone around her that she would do anything to be in that movie.

"I think the most important thing to get ahead falls back to what I truly believe in and that is the ability to seek truth in your life. And that's in all forms. You have to be honest with yourself."
Oprah Winfrey[39]

Oprah believes (as do I) that the events in her life that had led her to this exact place in her career, combined with her desire to be in *The Color Purple*, is what manifested great change.

---

[39] "Young Oprah Winfrey interview on her Life and Career." 44:57. YouTube.

"You are responsible for your life. That although there may be tragedy in your life, there's always a possibility to triumph. Doesn't matter who you are, where you come from. And that the ability to triumph begins with you, always. Always."
Oprah Winfrey[40]

Quincy Jones was one of the producers of *The Color Purple*, along with Frank Marshall, Kathleen Kennedy and Steven Spielberg. Quincy was in a hotel in Chicago in 1985 when he saw Oprah on AM Chicago. It was in this moment that he knew that he had found Sofia.

Quincy Jones discovered Oprah. Oprah auditioned for the role of Sofia in her favorite book-turned-movie, and the rest is history. She went on to be nominated for an Academy Award for Best Actress in a Supporting Role as Sofia in *The Color Purple*.

This was her first acting role, ever. *Ever!*
To walk away with a nomination from The Academy of Motion Picture Arts and Sciences is beyond unimaginable, yet it happened.

While filming *The Color Purple* she asked for time off to sign the deal for syndication of her new talk show.

---

[40] "Young Oprah Winfrey interview on her Life and Career." 24:00. YouTube.

*"I think if you're on the road to success,
is if you would do your job and not be paid for it.
That's how you know you're doing the right thing."*
Oprah Winfrey[41]

She used the platform on her talk show to inspire and to promote positive change in viewers around the world. Oprah has always wanted to make a difference in the lives of other people and in my opinion, she's achieved that goal, one hundred times over.

The Oprah Winfrey Show aired nationally in 1986 and remained on the air for 25 seasons. Around 40 million viewers tuned in to watch *The Oprah Winfrey Show* every week across America. She attributes her success in life to staying true to herself.

*"I am where I am today because I have
allowed myself to listen to my feelings."*
Oprah Winfrey[42]

Oprah has served as an inspiration to millions of people across America and around the globe. She continues to surprise and inspire viewers today through her television network *OWN (The Oprah Winfrey Network)* and the Emmy® award-winning, *Super Soul Sunday*, which airs on OWN.

---

[41] "Young Oprah Winfrey interview on her Life and Career." 58:44. YouTube.
[42] "Young Oprah Winfrey interview on her Life and Career." 39:40. YouTube.

Former president of the United States, Barack Obama, speaking to Oprah on *The Oprah Winfrey Show*:

"...I just want you to know that you have changed this country in unimaginable ways and it just has to do with what folks were just saying. You've got a big heart and you share it with people and nobody knows how to connect better than you do. And so we are just blessed and grateful to have you in our lives."
Barack Obama[43]

Chain of Events

Oprah learned how to read from her grandmother. She always had an interest in speaking which led her to give public speeches at the young age of three and a half years old.

As a teenager, she did an interview with a local radio station. The same person who conducted that interview later remembered Oprah and asked if she would represent his radio station during the Miss Fire Prevention Contest.

Oprah attributes her candid and open honesty during the contest to her winning. After winning the

---

[43] "Oprah, President Obama And First Lady Michelle Obama." 42:10. YouTube.

contest, she was asked casually if she'd like to hear her voice on tape back at the station. When the radio station heard how well she read, she was hired on the spot. This became her first job in the entertainment industry.

Her job at the radio station led to someone hearing her on the radio and then offering her a job in television.

After she got the television job, Quincy Jones saw her on T.V. and said that he had found Sofia for the movie he was a producer on, *The Color Purple*, which was also Oprah's favorite book.

She was nominated for an Academy Award for Best Actress in a Supporting Role for her role as Sofia in *The Color Purple*. Gaining some notoriety, she would go on to host a nationally syndicated talk show, *The Oprah Winfrey Show*, and the rest is history.

◆

The quote from Oprah, "I don't believe in luck, I think luck is preparation meeting opportunity," has really resonated with me. It's such a simple, yet powerful message that seems to sum up so many events in her life perfectly.

She practiced her speaking throughout her youth and accepted major opportunities that came her way, but many of those opportunities she created for herself. Each opportunity was built on the previous one. She kept placing herself in the line of sight of success and was pleasantly surprised when success followed.

It's an inspiring story from an inspirational woman who I've admired for many years. During her acceptance speech for the Jean Hersholt Humanitarian Award in 2011, she described her success as being "unimaginable".[44] It's a powerful speech I think everyone should watch at least once.

Watching successful people live their lives when you yourself do not feel successful can make that success feel *unimaginable*.

Maybe you don't have to know every step of the journey, but continuously following your dreams and placing yourself in the line of sight of success can take you to that unimaginable place.

It has happened to people before and it can happen to you, too. Stay true to yourself and do the things that you truly love, and the rest will follow.

---

[44] "Oprah Winfrey accepts her Jean Hersholt Humanitarian Award." 02:00. YouTube.

Writer I Stephen King

Stephen King, one of America's most prolific writers of our time, has had a successful career spanning 50 years.

Many of his books have been made into movies or T.V. series, including *Carrie, Children of the Corn, It, Cujo, The Green Mile, Stand By Me,* and *Misery.*

He has either produced, written, or acted in, sometimes all three, in 30+ productions. He's directed films and has even made his way into the music industry by creating an intro to a song by the band Blue Oyster Cult.

Stephen King Has Received a Multitude of Awards and Honors

He's won multiple lifetime achievement awards, from The Audio Publishers Association,[45] Canadian Booksellers Association,[46] Horror Writers Association,[47] and from the World Fantasy Awards.[48]

He won the 2003 National Book Foundation Medal for Distinguished Contribution to American Letters.[49]

---

[45] "2020 AUDIE AWARDS - STEPHEN KING." The Audio Publishers Association (APA).

[46] "Booksellers honour 'heavy metal' King of writing." CBC.

[47] "Lifetime Achievement Award." Horror Writers Association.

[48] "Winners." World Fantasy Convention.

[49] "Stephen King - Medal for Distinguished Contribution to American Letters." National Book Award.

He won the 2014 National Medal of Arts.[50] This is "the highest award given to artists and arts patrons by the United States government" and was awarded by President Barack Obama.[51]

He received The World Horror Society's Grand Master Award in 1992 from the World Horror Convention.[52]

Stephen received the Grand Master Award from the Mystery Writers of America in 2007.[53]

He received the Alumni Career Award from the University of Maine in 1981.[54] Overall, Stephen King has won 100+ awards for his contribution to the literary world.[55]

Humble Beginnings

When you consider Stephen King's massive body of work, along with the countless awards and accolades he's received throughout his career, you might think he was just born into it, always having success and never

---

[50] "Stephen King." National Endowment for the Arts.

[51] "Accepts Nominations for 2021 National Medal of Arts." National Endowment for the Arts.

[52] "WHC - Grand Master." World Horror Convention.

[53] "Category List – The Grand Master." The Edgar Awards.

[54] "Alumni Career Award." UMaine Alumni Association.

[55] King, Tabitha. "The Author." Stephen King.

knowing anything else. This couldn't be further from the truth.

Stephen Edwin King was born in Maine on September 21st, 1947. He and his brother David were raised by their mother Nellie. Their father left the family when Stephen was two years old. Stephen never met his father, who passed away in 1980.

Stephen was an avid reader, even from a young age. His mother loved to read and would read stories like *Doctor Jekyll and Mr. Hyde* to Stephen and David when they were just six and eight years old.

Stephen enjoyed writing short stories in school and would contribute them to the school newspaper. At some point, he knew he wanted to earn a living as a writer. He would type on his old typewriter and began sending his stories to magazines in the hope that they'd be published.

That's when the rejection slips started to roll in. For each rejection slip he received, he would nail it into the wall. By the time he was around 18 years old, he'd received so many rejections that the nail fell out of the wall.

"If there's any, any secret that I know to success it's, if you don't succeed get a bigger nail."
Stephen King[56]

---

[56] "Stephen King - secret to his success." 01:02. YouTube.

He went on to receive his Bachelor of Arts in English from the University of Maine in 1970. With his degree, he was able to teach English at high school level. He continued to write while at home and during school year holidays and vacations.

He met his wife Tabitha, "...in the stacks of the Fogler Library at the University of Maine at Orono, where they both worked as students."[57]
They got married in 1971 while Stephen was working at a gas station and Tabitha was still in school and had two children soon after.

When Stephen found it difficult to find work as a teacher, he made ends meet working at a laundromat while Tabitha was working at Dunkin' Donuts. He eventually got a teaching job earning him $6,400 a year.

Even through the financial challenges the family was facing, he remembers thinking during this time regarding his relationship with Tabby, "I'm not going to leave this marriage no matter what happens."[58]

---

[57] King, Tabitha. "The Author." Stephen King.

[58] Greene. "Stephen King: The Rolling Stone Interview." Rolling Stone.

"So, I would teach school, come home, she'd work at
Dunkin' Donuts. I would baby-sit the kids and give them
the bottles and change them and everything until she
came
home at 11.00. And then we'd go to bed."
Stephen King[59]

He was able to sell short stories to magazines. Primarily
men's X-rated magazines. But, it was a paycheck and he
had a family to support, so he welcomed the work. He
was happy to have this extra income and was also proud
that his work was actually being published.

He wanted to show his published works to his
mother, so his wife who worked at the Foghorn Library
would photocopy his stories, covering up any parts of the
magazine that, let's say, weren't relevant to the tales
being told.

Stephen began writing novels and while he was
teaching, he came up with a great idea for one.
When you're a teacher and a father of two, you don't
have a whole lot of time for yourself, so Stephen decided
to use the full 10-day vacation during the February
school break to finish the novel *The Running Man*.

He recalls sending it out to a science fiction
publisher. Stephen received a response from the
publisher, "...there is no market for dystopian fantasies."[60]

---

[59] Greene."Stephen King: The Rolling Stone Interview." Rolling Stone.

When you consider the fact that Stephen's incredibly successful career is filled with dystopian fantasies, it really makes you question the validity of some rejections one may receive.

The Running Man wasn't the book that would end up putting Stephen King on the map. It would be years until this book would be published and when it was, it was published under the pseudonym Richard Bachman.

Stephen, undeterred, continued writing and decided to start working on a new story, Carrie. Carrie started as a short story, but it had grown too long to be sold to the men's magazines that Stephen had been selling his stories to. The finished novel was 199 pages. He didn't know how he could sell it, so he threw it away, literally.

"I was teaching, and that presented a problem for me, and the money constraints presented a problem, so I threw Carrie away and my wife fished it out of the wastebasket and said, 'You ought a go on.'"
Stephen King[61]

He decided to take his wife's advice and finish Carrie. One day while Stephen was at work, teaching at school,

---

60 "Stephen King reveals the secret to his success." 03:25. YouTube.

61 "Carrie: Rescued from the Bin | Mark Lawson Talks to Stephen King" 02:00. YouTube.

he was in the teachers' room when he heard an announcement made over the school loudspeakers, "Stephen King, please come to the office, you have an urgent call from your wife. And I knew going up that either a kid had broken his leg, or I sold the book. And it was the book."[62]

The couple didn't even have a working telephone line to receive the good news on as they'd had it disconnected to save money.

"We didn't have a phone...We had to let something go in order to continue to pay for, you know the baby food and the baby medicine and everything. We had to economize."
Stephen King[63]

That's why the editor had to send a telegram to the house, letting Stephen know the book had been sold. The telegram also informed Stephen that he'd be receiving an advance of $2,500 for *Carrie*.

"It sold as a novel. It's a skinny little thing, but it made me what I am today."
Stephen King[64]

---

[62] "Talking Volumes: Stephen King on 'Carrie.'" 02:08. YouTube.
[63] "Talking Volumes: Stephen King on 'Carrie.'" 01:36. YouTube.
[64] "Talking Volumes: Stephen King on 'Carrie.'" 01:22. YouTube.

With the advance, Stephen and Tabitha traded in their old car for a brand-new Ford Pinto. They were very happy about the new car, the fact that it had the potential to explode was just a side note.

The most Stephen had ever made from one of his short stories up to that point was $500. An advance of $2,500 was a giant leap in the right direction. There was to be a paperback sale of the book. Stephen and the publishing company would split profits 50/50. He expected and hoped that the sale of the book would allow him to take a year off from teaching. This would give him space and time to write another book. He thought that the book could sell for up to $60,000, which would make his cut $30,000. It went on to sell for $400,000.

"I got that news from my editor on a Sunday. My wife was up visiting her mother and I was in the house, she'd taken the kids, I was there by myself, and my legs went out from under me…I finally decided I had to buy my wife a present. It was Sunday, everything was closed, except for LaVerdiere's
drug store so I bought her a hair dryer."
Stephen King[65]

Stephen King went on to publish 200+ written works between 1974 and 1999.

---

[65] "Talking Volumes: Stephen King on 'Carrie.'" 04:00. YouTube.

On June 19th, 1999, Stephen left the house to take his daily 4-mile walk.

"I was walking up the side of the road, on the shoulder, and something came over the top very fast and I thought to myself 'It's a school bus that's gonna hit me.'"
Stephen King[66]

It wasn't a school bus that hit Stephen, but a Dodge Caravan being driven by a distracted driver who was dealing with his dogs in the backseat. He drove completely off the road and onto the shoulder where Stephen was walking. Stephen hit the windshield and flew over the roof. He clung to consciousness after being hit and was rushed to the hospital.

This accident left him with his right leg, knee and hip, all completely shattered. His lung was on the brink of collapsing, he had multiple broken ribs, tibial fractures in at least nine places, and part of his scalp had been torn away.

He went on to have eight operations and suffered through five months of excruciating physical therapy. Even after all this, his right leg was still being held together by pins. Doctors weren't sure if he'd ever regain full use of that leg again.

It was incredibly difficult for Stephen to write again after the accident.

---

[66] "Stephen King Interview - The Today Show" 01:24. YouTube.

*"There was this one awful minute where I sat there
and thought 'I can't do this; I don't know
how to do this anymore.'"*
Stephen King[67]

He wasn't sure if it was a memory or confidence issue,
but eventually he decided to come back to writing.

*"...at first, it was as if I had never done this in my life. It
was like starting over again from square one."*
Stephen King[68]

He was in a tremendous amount of pain and sitting at a
desk for long periods of time wasn't even an option for
him. At one point he said, "Maybe there will be another
book, maybe there won't. Today I'm more concerned with
walking again without crutches."[69]

Writing has always been an escape for Stephen.
An escape into another world that, as he writes, becomes
as real to him as the world we all live in. Although it took
some time, he would go on to write again.

The first book he wrote after his accident was
Dreamcatcher. Dreamcatcher was published on February

---

[67] Stephen King Interview - The Today Show" 04:50. YouTube.

[68] Stephen King Interview - The Today Show" 04:40. YouTube.

[69] Stephen King Interview - The Today Show" 00:50. YouTube.

20th, 2001. Since its publication, Stephen has had 150+ published written works.

Stephen King's career includes 350+ published written works, countless movies and adaptations of his stories, awards, accolades, and recognition from his fans and peers as being one of the most prolific writers of our generation.

Chain of Events

Stephen King always loved reading and writing. He contributed stories to his school newspaper at a young age and began sending his short stories to magazines in high school, in the hopes that they'd be published and that he'd be compensated for his work.

He met his wife Tabitha at the University of Maine, where they were both attending. He received his Bachelor of Arts in English in 1970 and married Tabitha in 1971. Soon after, they had two children.

He had trouble finding a job as a teacher, so he worked at a laundromat while Tabitha worked at Dunkin' Donuts, all while raising two small children together.

Stephen earned supplementary income selling short stories to men's X-rated magazines. He eventually landed a teaching job.

While teaching, he wrote Carrie, a 199-page novel. Since he didn't think any of the men's magazines would publish it, he literally threw Carrie in the garbage.

Tabitha "fished it out of the wastebasket and said, 'You ought a go on.'" Through her encouragement to finish *Carrie*, the novel went on to get published and earn $400,000 at the time.
This allowed him to quit teaching and focus on writing entirely.

◆

When you take into consideration what Stephen and Tabitha's lives looked like before *Carrie*, it's an incredible transformation. But, not one that happened overnight.

My favorite quote of Stephen King's is, "If there's any secret that I know to success, it's if you don't succeed, get a bigger nail." He faced rejection from so many people in high places, but he never let that slow him down.

Because of his resilience and tenacity, he was able to push on and become one of the most well-known authors in the world.

Actress | Kate Winslet

Kate Elisabeth Winslet is an actress best-known for the unforgettable and eclectic roles she's taken on throughout her career.

A career that began at age seven when only her left arm made an on-screen debut during a commercial for Sugar Puffs, now includes 50+ leading roles in films and television series alike.

She's been a producer on multiple projects and has even proven to be a talented singer as well as actress, having a hit song reach #6 on the Official U.K. Top 10 Chart.[70]

She's won over 90 awards and has received over 150+ nominations for her outstanding work in film and television. She's even won a Grammy for Best Spoken Word Album for Children for *Listen to the Storyteller.*[71]

She's a prolific actress who has had a profound impact on the entertainment industry. Arguably one of the greatest actresses of our generation, Kate has proven that anything is possible, and dreams really do come true.

---

[70] "KATE WINSLET | full Official Chart History."Official Charts.

[71] "Kate Winslet | Artist."GRAMMY.com.

Kate Winslet Has Received a Multitude of Awards and Honors

Kate won the Academy Award for her role in *The Reader*.[72] She's been nominated six other times for her roles in *Titanic, Eternal Sunshine of the Spotless Mind, Sense and Sensibility, Iris, Little Children* and *Steve Jobs*.[73]

She's won four Golden Globes to date. In 2009 she was awarded two Golden Globes for her roles in *Revolutionary Road* and *The Reader*. She also received Golden Globes for her role in *Mildred Pierce* and in *Steve Jobs*. She's received seven additional Golden Globe nominations.[74]

She's the winner of the two Primetime Emmy® Awards. The first was awarded to Kate in 2011 for Outstanding Lead Actress In A Miniseries Or A Movie for playing Mildred Pierce in *Mildred Pierce*. The other was received more recently, in 2021 for her outstanding role in *Mare of Easttown*. She was even nominated for an Emmy® in 2006 for Outstanding Guest Actress In A

---

[72] "Kate Winslet Academy Awards Acceptance Speech." Oscar speech database.

[73] "Kate Winslet - Awards." IMDb.

[74] "Kate Winslet." Golden Globes.

Comedy Series, where she played herself on the show *Extras*.[75]

She's won three BAFTA Awards for her work in *Steve Jobs*, *The Reader*, and *Sense and Sensibility* and also received nominations for her work in *Eternal Sunshine of The Spotless Mind*, *Finding Neverland*, *Iris*, and *Little Children*. She also won The Britannia Award for British Artist of the Year in 2007.[76]

She received "...British Actress prize in celebration of her film career..." from Harper's Bazaar.[77]

Kate has received multiple awards from the Screen Actors Guild,[78] as well as international recognition from the Australian Academy of Cinema and Television Arts,[79] the British Independent Film Awards,[80] and the European Film Awards,[81] to name a few.

In 2014 The Hollywood Chamber of Commerce honored Kate Winslet with a star on the famous Walk of Fame in Hollywood, California.[82]

---

[75] "Kate Winslet - Emmy Awards, Nominations and Wins." Television Academy.

[76] "BAFTA Awards Search | BAFTA Awards." BAFTA.

[77] "Kate Winslet - Women Of The Year Awards."Independent.ie.

[78] "Nominations Announced for the 22nd Annual Screen Actors Guild Awards." Screen Actors Guild Awards.

[79] "Winners & Nominees | 5th AACTA Awards." AACTA.

[80] "Kate Winslet to receive The Variety Award." BIFA.

[81] "Titanic - Film." European Film Awards.

[82] "Kate Winslet." Hollywood Walk of Fame.

Humble Beginnings

Growing up in a family of actors may have introduced Kate to the world of acting, but her family's connections didn't make the journey from Reading, England to Hollywood, California any easier.

Kate Winslet was born and raised in Reading, England, on October 5th, 1975. Putting on shows was commonplace in the Winslet household between Kate, her two sisters, and brother. Her mom worked in the local sandwich shop and her dad did everything from selling Christmas trees to delivering mail between acting gigs.

There wasn't a VCR in the house until Kate was 15 years old, but the few movies she did watch combined with her family's love for acting left enough of an imprint on her to want to do the same. Kate wanted to be Sandy from Grease and she wasn't going to let anyone stand in her way!

"I wanted to be an actress, and
nothing was going to stop me."
Kate Winslet[83]

From a young age, Kate had to overcome adversity, from bullies at school to teachers putting her down, there were many large hurdles to get where she is today.

---

[83] "Kate Winslet's - WE Day." 05:05. YouTube.

Kate was teased at school by her classmates over her weight. One student was particularly cruel to Kate. On one occasion, when Kate arrived back at school on a Monday, the classroom that had been completely rearranged. She found her desk had been moved to one corner of the classroom and all of the other students' desks were moved to the other side of the room.

She didn't know that she was walking into "not talk to Kate day."[84] All of this was done by one classmate who just didn't like Kate and intentionally went out of her way to upset her any way she could.

"If you've ever been put down, or told that you're not good enough, first of all, ignore it and use that fuel to push you on towards your dreams."
Kate Winslet[85]

To be teased by immature children is one thing, but to hear cruel and discouraging words from your own teachers is another.

---

[84] "Conan O'Brien 'Kate Winslet." 06:25. YouTube.
[85] "Kate Winslet's - WE Day." 00:33. YouTube.

"I was told by a drama teacher that I might do okay if I was happy to settle for the fat girl parts. Look at me now. Look at me now. And so, what I feel like saying in those moments to any young woman who has ever been put down by a teacher or a friend or even a parent, just don't listen to any of it, because that's what I did. I didn't listen and I kept on going and I overcame all of my fears, and I got over a lot of insecurity and just keep doing it and keep believing in yourself."
Kate Winslet[86]

Kate's ability to tune out these lies truly speaks to her strength, the confidence she has in knowing who she is, what she's capable of, and her determination to do what will make her the happiest. Despite what others may think.

"I would rarely hear anything positive. So, I started to feel uncomfortable in my own skin. It made it hard. I wanted to give up. 'Maybe I should rethink this acting thing' I said to myself. But, it was my passion and it made me happy!" Kate Winslet[87]

Kate carried on doing plays and musicals as a teenager. When she was 16 years old, she left school and worked at a delicatessen. This was the same place where most

[86] Bailey. "Kate Winslet BAFTA Speech - Kate Winslet on Self Doubt." ELLE.
[87] "Kate Winslet's - WE Day." 04:20. YouTube.

of her family members had worked at one time or another. She worked there to earn enough money so she could afford the train fare to travel to London, where she would go on auditions.

The movie *Heavenly Creatures*, which would be Kate's break-out role, was based on the real-life story of two young girls who share a strong bond that motivates them to commit a terrible act of violence.

A casting director was sent to the U.K. to find a girl who looked similar to Juliet Hulme. Kate Winslet was invited to audition for the role.

As she and her father drove to pick up the script for the audition, Kate recalls asking him if he thought she would get the role. She remembers he just looked at her and said, "Yeah, you will."[88]

"I remember thinking. 'God that's it isn't it! I've got to absolutely believe that I'm gonna get this part,' because so much of it is believing that you will and willing things into existence and I do remember thinking, 'Okay I'm going to go in there and I'm going to, I'm just somehow going to give them no option but to give me this part.'"
Kate Winslet[89]

---

[88] "Kate Winslet: A Life In Pictures." 02:10. YouTube.

[89] "Kate Winslet: A Life In Pictures." 02:25. YouTube.

She auditioned for the role, but didn't get it right away. She followed that audition with four more before being offered the part months later.

Kate was actually in the middle of making a turkey sandwich for a customer at the deli where she was working when she heard the phone ring.

"...it was the strangest thing, there was something about the way the phone rang that I remember thinking 'It's for me!'"
Kate Winslet[90]

Kate's child agent was on the line, congratulating her for landing the role of Juliet Hulme in Peter Jackson's new film *Heavenly Creatures*. This would be the first film of many that would land Kate Winslet worldwide recognition and acclaim.

It was only a year and a half later that Kate would go on a casting call and land the role of Marianne Dashwood in *Sense and Sensibility*, directed by Ang Lee. This was Kate's second film.

The first day of shooting *Sense and Sensibility* was coming to an end. Since Ang Lee had barely spoken to Kate all day, she was a bit concerned that maybe he wasn't happy with her performance. She wanted to know what he thought of her work so far, so she asked him,

---

[90] "Kate Winslet Dropped Out Of School At 16." 02:45. YouTube.

"How was everything?" and he told her "You'll get better."[91]

Although Kate has an extraordinary way of making the roles she takes on seem effortless, that doesn't mean that she hasn't faced difficulties along the way. Even the incredibly talented Kate Winslet has experienced self-doubt and uncertainty.

"Don't be afraid to make mistakes,
you will only learn from them."
Kate Winslet[92]

A rocky start, but *Sense and Sensibility* ended up being the role that would give Kate her first Oscar nomination as Best Actress in a Supporting Role and her first Golden Globe nomination for Best Performance by an Actress in a Supporting Role in a Motion Picture.
The film took home 33 wins and 49 nominations.
Kate Winslet walked away with five awards for her role in the film.

Kate delivered extraordinary performances in these two roles which led to future roles in *Jude* and *Hamlet* the following year, 1996. *Jude* went on to receive 5 awards and 6 nominations and *Hamlet* received 9 awards and 25 nominations. Two more incredible

---

[91] "Kate Winslet: A Life In Pictures." 08:42. YouTube.

[92] "Kate Winslet's - WE Day." 12:05. YouTube.

performances by Kate Winslet in two films that were also very well received.

"You can be from anywhere and
you can do anything. Believe it"
Kate Winslet[93]

Some actresses may have been intimidated to work with famous directors at such a young age and also at the start of their careers, but this never stopped Kate.

She spent a lot of time developing the characters she was set to play. She researched her roles extensively, preparing herself as much as possible so when the cameras started rolling, she'd be ready, and she always was.

"You have to be indestructible to do what you love
and believe that you are worth it."
Kate Winslet[94]

When Kate heard about the movie *Titanic* that was being directed by James Cameron, she knew that she had what it would take to play Rose and just needed to be given the chance. Kate spoke with James and told him how much she loved the role and that she believed she could do it.

---

[93] "Kate Winslet's - WE Day." 06:50. YouTube.
[94] "Kate Winslet's - WE Day." 05:30. YouTube.

"She sent me a rose with a note that
basically said, 'I'm ready.'"
James Cameron[95]

It was her tenacity, the unwavering belief she had in
herself, and her outstanding acting abilities that landed
her the role after reading with multiple potential male
leads.

Titanic would be the fifth movie she would film
after *Heavenly Creatures*. It went on to reach
international recognition and has become one of the
most beloved love stories of all time.

Titanic has won 125 awards and has received 83
nominations.[96] Kate took home seven awards for her role
as Rose Dewitt Bukater in *Titanic*.[97]

After experiencing the success of *Titanic*, Kate
was offered a plethora of roles. She declined almost all of
them, recalling feeling unready for certain parts. She
wanted to take a step away from the limelight and focus
on the craft itself, on acting, which is what she's always
loved and has been the most passionate about.

She had a strong desire to improve her acting
abilities even further, which is why she followed *Titanic*,
which was a major commercial success, with films like

---

[95] "Kate Winslet's first Titanic screen test." 00:05. YouTube.
[96] "Titanic (1997) - Awards." IMDb.
[97] "Kate Winslet - Awards." IMDb.

Hideous Kinky and *Holy Smoke* that were smaller budget films, but were still received very well by audiences.

Kate Winslet has never played the same role twice. Each character she's chosen to portray has been unlike any others she's ever played before.
From *Heavenly Creatures* to *Titanic* to *Hamlet* and *Holy Smoke*, Kate has proven that she can perform a wide range of characters, seemingly effortlessly.

She's mentioned that her favorite role that she's ever played was that of Clementine Kruczynski in *Eternal Sunshine of the Spotless Mind*, but the role that she's the most proud of playing would be one that she took on in 2008 as Hanna Schmitz in *The Reader*.

It would be her role in *The Reader* that would win Kate her first Oscar for Best Performance by an Actress in a Leading Role after being nominated for five other roles.

"I'd be lying if I haven't made a version of this speech before. I think I was probably eight years old looking into the bathroom mirror and this (holding the Oscar) would have been a shampoo bottle. Well, it's not a shampoo bottle now."
Kate Winslet[98]

---

[98] "Kate Winslet winning Best Actress for "The Reader." 06:50. YouTube.

She continues to push the boundaries of what we believe one person may be capable of. Not only has she won nearly 100 awards within her industry, but she's worked alongside some of the biggest names in Hollywood and continues to do so to this day.

Kate is married to Edward Abel Smith and has three children. She's managed to have an incredibly prolific career while also being a mother of three. The grace, elegance, truth, and beauty that she brings to every single role she takes on is astounding. She's proven that anything is possible and that as long as you believe in yourself, there's nothing you can't achieve.

Chain of Events

Kate has always loved acting as a young girl growing up in Reading, England. Her left arm starred in a commercial for Sugar Puffs at age seven. This was her first acting role, technically.

From there, she performed in plays and musicals throughout high school when she would save up money in order to take the train to London for auditions.

She was offered to audition for the role of Juliet Hulme in *Heavenly Creatures,* directed by Peter Jackson. After multiple auditions for the role, she got the part, finding out the good news while in the middle of making a turkey sandwich for a customer at the deli where she worked. She delivered such a remarkable performance that she received multiple awards for her work in the film.

This would be her breakout role that would lead to her next role as Marianne Dashwood in *Sense and Sensibility,* directed by Ang Lee.

Again, Kate's performance was incredibly well received which led to her first Oscar nomination.

She went on to star in two more films, *Jude* and *Hamlet,* before convincing director James Cameron to give her the opportunity to play Rose in his new film *Titanic.* She sent a rose to James with a note attached that said, "I'm ready." And she was.

She read with multiple male leads before being chosen to play Rose Dewitt Bukater in a film that would become one of the highest-grossing films of all time.

After *Titanic,* she was offered every role under the sun, but decided instead to focus on developing her craft. Kate went on to perform in 50+ projects over the next two decades, all while being a wife and a mother of three.

President I Barack Obama

Barack Obama is now a household name, but that wasn't always the case.

Before Barack Hussein Obama II would become the first African American President of the United States, he was a Senator, a professor at the University of Chicago, and before that, he worked as a community organizer earning $13k a year.
He truly had humble beginnings which makes his story that much more compelling.

This young boy from Hawaii who was raised by a single mother would grow up to serve as a symbol of hope and inspiration to millions of people and countless generations around the world. Barack has proven that even a young person growing up in challenging circumstances can reach incredible heights and accomplish the seemingly impossible.

His path to the presidency was not an easy one. It was in fact, very unlikely that he would become the first African American President of the United States.
Barack overcame challenges that were presented to him and in doing so, paved his own path to the presidency.

Barack Obama Has Received a Multitude of Awards and Honors

Barack Obama was awarded the Nobel Peace Prize in 2009 "...for his extraordinary efforts to strengthen international diplomacy and cooperation between peoples."[99]

"It's an award that speaks to our highest aspirations. That for all the cruelty and hardship of our world, we are not mere prisoners of fate."
Barack Obama, on receiving the Nobel Peace Prize in 2009[100]

Barack was the recipient of the NAACP (National Association for the Advancement of Colored People) Chairman's Award in 2005.[101]

Barack Obama was awarded the Department of Defense Medal for Distinguished Public Service by The Secretary of Defense, "For distinguished public service as the Commander-in-Chief of the finest fighting force the world has ever known from January 20, 2009, to January 20, 2017." [102]

---

[99] "The Nobel Peace Prize for 2009 to President Barack Obama." Nobel Prize.

[100] "2009 Nobel Peace Prize Lecture by Barack Obama." 00:30. Youtube.

[101] "Sen. Barack Obama - 36th NAACP Image Awards - Chairman's Award." 00:35. YouTube.

[102] "THE UNITED STATES OF AMERICA." Department of Defense.

He received the John F. Kennedy Profile in Courage Award in 2017.[103]

Israel awarded Barack the Presidential Medal of Distinction in 2013, which is the country's highest honor.[104]

In 2014, Barack Obama received the, "Ambassador for Humanity" Award by the USC Shoah Foundation.[105]

FIRST (For Inspiration and Recognition of Science and Technology) honored Barack Obama in 2017 with the "Make It Loud" Award, "...for his significant contributions to raising awareness about FIRST among the general public and helping spread the mission and impact of the organization."[106]

Barack won the Hero of the Year Award at Shockwaves NME Awards in 2009.[107]

He's won two Grammys for Best Spoken Word Albums for *The Audacity of Hope: Thoughts on*

[103] "President Barack Obama Receives 2017 Centennial John F. Kennedy Profile in Courage Award." JFK Library.

[104] "Obama to receive special award in Israel." USA Today.

[105] Grossberg. "President Obama honored by USC Shoah Foundation." USC News.

[106] "FIRST Honors President Barack Obama" FIRST Inspires.

[107] "Shockwaves NME Awards 2009: The Winners." NME.

Reclaiming the American Dream in 2007 and for the album *Dreams from My Father* in 2005.[108]

He's also in The Wilderness Hall of Fame: "Put simply, few presidents — if any — have done as much as President Obama did to safeguard our planet and our country for future generations. He is a thoroughly deserving inductee into the Wilderness Hall of Fame, and a figure whom other leaders present and future would do well to emulate."[109]

Humble Beginnings

Barack Hussein Obama II, or more commonly known as Barack Obama, is the 44th president of the United States of America. Barack was born on August 4th, 1961, in Honolulu, Hawaii.

Barack's parents met in Hawaii. His mom, Stanley Ann Dunham, was a white woman from Kansas who moved to Hawaii in 1959 with her parents. Barack's father, Barack Obama Sr., was an African American originally from Kenya. Barack Sr. met Ann at the University of Hawaii in 1960.

---

[108] "Barack Obama | Artist."GRAMMY.com.

[109] "The Wilderness Hall of Fame: 13 presidents who were true conservation leaders." The Wilderness Society.

Barack's mother was named Stanley since her father originally wanted to have a son. However, she would go by her middle name Ann for most of her life.

Barack Sr. was able to attend the University of Hawaii on a scholarship. He was the first African American student at the University of Hawaii.

Barack's parents met while they were both in the same Russian class when Barack Sr. was 25 and Ann was 17. The two dated for a short time before Ann found out she was pregnant.

Ann was three months pregnant with Barack when she and Barack Senior got married. But, unfortunately, there were things Ann didn't know about Barack Sr.'s life in Kenya, such as the fact that her now-husband was actually already married to a woman back in Kenya, Kezia Obama. To make matters worse, it turned out that he had a son with Kezia and even had another child on the way.

Barack and Ann stayed together for some time. Ann dropped out of school to take care of Barack while Barack Sr. went on to graduate. It would be a short-lived marriage.

"My father, I only met him once for a month when I was 10. I probably was shaped more by his absence than his presence."
Barack Obama[110]

Barack was only two years old when his parents got divorced. Barack's mother Ann struggled financially and was even on food stamps at one point while raising Barack. But, she was a single mom who was passionate about education and instilling the right values in Barack from an early age.

Ann would soon fall in love with and marry an Indonesian student, Soetoro Martodihardjo who went by the name Lolo Soetoro. They got married in 1965 and when Barack was six years old, he, his mom and her new husband Lolo, moved to Indonesia.

There were some challenges facing the family after moving to Indonesia. They faced financial hardships and couldn't even afford a refrigerator in their new home.

Aside from financial difficulties, Barack, being an African American boy in Indonesia, stood out amongst his classmates. He was often teased by other children who just didn't see that many African American students at school.

Since education was always very important to Ann, she sent Barack to the best schools she could in

---

[110] "American Stories, American Solutions: 30 Minute Special." 15:43. YouTube.

Indonesia and would even help him study before and after school.

Ann would wake Barack up at 4.30 in the morning to help him with his studies before school began. Barack, being a young child at the time, wasn't exactly thrilled to start his day this early. When he would grumble, she would remind him, "This is no picnic for me either, Buster."[111]

Despite the difficulties that came with moving to a new country with limited funds, things did improve over time. Lolo eventually got a higher paying job, which allowed the family to move to a nicer home in a better neighborhood.

Ann's interests were in philanthropic ventures across Indonesia, Pakistan and the United States. She focused on women's work and supporting rural farmers. Ann spoke fluent Bahasa Indonesian and had a selfless interest in improving the lives of others.

"She joined Indonesia's oldest bank to work on what was described as the world's largest sustainable microfinance program to assist poor farmers and rural entrepreneurs with credit and savings projects."[112]

In Indonesia, Ann would have her second child, Barack's half-sister Maya on August 15th, 1970. Barack was nine years old when Maya was born.

---

[111] "Pres. Obama National Address to Students." 02:16. YouTube.

[112] Bender. "Legacy of the President's Mother: Ann Dunham" University of Hawaii System.

Ann made the difficult decision of sending Barack back to Hawaii to live with his grandparents when he was 10 years old with the hopes that he would receive a better education. Barack became very close to his grandparents.

"She's the one who taught me about hard work. She's the one who put off buying a new car or a new dress for herself so that I could have a better life. She poured everything she had into me."
Barack Obama speaking about his grandmother[113]

For Barack, this would be a challenging time. Since there was again, a small African American population where he was living in Hawaii at the time, he had some negative interactions relating to race that he would later discuss at length in his first published book *Dreams from My Father*.

This was a challenging time for Ann as well, who was raising her newborn daughter Maya while also working in order to pay for schooling for both of her children. Ann's parents essentially raised Barack during this time. Ann and Maya would join Barack in Hawaii in 1972.

When he was 10, Barack's father was visiting Hawaii and he had the opportunity to meet him. This would be the only memory he would have of his father,

---

[113] Nasaw. "Obama pauses campaign to visit ailing grandmother" The Guardian.

who was later killed in an automobile accident in Kenya. Barack was a senior at Columbia University when he received the news.

Ann, Maya and Barack remained in Hawaii for the following three years. During this time, Ann continued her studies as a graduate student at the University of Hawaii. Barack would soon be entering high school and preferred to finish his studies in Hawaii.

The family separated again as Ann returned to Indonesia with Maya, while Barack remained in Hawaii to finish his studies with his grandparents. Even during these times of separation, Ann and Barack remained very close and were always in contact with one another.

Ann's marriage to Lolo ended in 1980, and she returned to Hawaii with Maya where she'd eventually go back to school to receive her PhD in anthropology.[114]

With the help of scholarships and student loans, Barack went on to attend some of the most prestigious schools in the world. He studied at Occidental College in Los Angeles, California in 1979. He transferred to Columbia University in New York City, New York during his sophomore year where he graduated with a Bachelor of Arts Degree in Political Science in 1983.

After graduating from Columbia, Barack was offered a job with a church-based group in Chicago where he worked as a community organizer.

---

[114] "Barack Obama's Mother." University of Washington.

"I loaded up all my belongings in this raggedy old car, and I drove out to Chicago. Didn't know a soul at the time."
Barack Obama[115]

Once in Chicago he helped set up job training for the unemployed. It was during a time when there was high unemployment in Chicago, so his presence and hard work was surely needed. The job only paid $13k a year, but it was Barack's first introduction to Chicago, a city that he would call home for many years to come.

He worked in this role for three years before applying and being accepted into Harvard Law School in 1988. He was only studying at Harvard for one year before he was an editor of the Harvard Law Review. The Harvard Law Review is, "...a student-run organization whose primary purpose is to publish a journal of legal scholarship."[116] It would only be one year later when Barack would be elected as the first black president of the Harvard Law Review.

Barack's time at Harvard would bring him many things. The prestige of being accepted into one of the best universities in the world, the reputation of being an accomplished student, and one who will go down in history as being the first African American to be elected

---

[115] Samuels. "Barack Obama, The Invisible Man." CBS News.
[116] "About the Harvard Law Review."Harvard Law Review.

president of the Harvard Law Review. Barack even graduated *magna cum laude* from Harvard Law School in 1991.

But perhaps the greatest thing that his time at Harvard brought him was the meeting of his future wife, Michelle. An African American woman who grew up on the South Side of Chicago, Michelle was 25 years old when she was first introduced to Barack.

She was working at a law firm in Chicago which ran a summer program that Barack had enrolled in. She was assigned as his mentor.

By this time, Michelle had already graduated *cum laude* from Princeton University and received her Juris Doctor degree from Harvard Law School. She was now a lawyer. Since the two had the Harvard connection, the firm thought they would be a good match. Turns out, they were right.

They had known each other for about a month before Barack asked Michelle out on a date. She was hesitant at first, but eventually she gave Barack a chance.

He took her to a training that was happening in a church basement where he was speaking.
The people who attended the training were mainly there because they had or were experiencing feelings of hopelessness in their lives.

"We walk in, and he takes off his suit jacket and launches
into what I think is the most eloquent discussion about
the world as it is and the world as it should be and that
was it.
Really after that day, that was it,
I was in love with him."
Michelle Obama[117]

They eventually made their way to an ice cream shop,
Baskin-Robbins in Hyde Park, a neighborhood in
Chicago.

It was here Barack and Michelle would share their
first kiss. Today, a plaque lives at this location.

"On our first date, I treated her to the finest ice cream
Baskin Robbins had to offer, our dinner table doubling
as the curb. I kissed her, and it tasted like chocolate."
Barack Obama[118]

Michelle and Barack didn't have much money at the time,
but they didn't let their financial struggles stand in the
way of their true love. Michelle recalls the car that Barack
had in the early days of their relationship. She
remembered how she could actually see the road under
her feet as they'd drive.

---

[117] "A Mother's Promise: Barack's Biography." 04:20. YouTube.
[118] "Barack and Michelle Obama's First Date - Famous Firsts." Oprah.com.

A hole had been created near the passenger-side of the car from rust eating through the steel of the frame. This was the car he was driving before they got married.

They had discussed the possibility of getting married, but Barack was playing it cool. The couple were at dinner celebrating him passing the Bar exam, when Barack decided to pick a fight with Michelle over getting married.

He was making a strong argument against getting married and Michelle took the opposing stance. Finally, it was time for dessert. The waiter brought out a small plate with a black box on it.

Barack opened the box and said, "Now that ought to shut you up."[119]

They got married on October 3rd, 1992.

"I had a pile of student loans at the time. I just married Michelle; she had a pile of student loans at the time."
Barack Obama[120] ·

Since the Obamas couldn't afford a place of their own quite yet, Barack moved into Michelle's parents' house in Chicago.

Between 1992 and 2004 Barack worked as a Constitutional professor at the University of Chicago. In 1995 Barack published his first book, *Dreams from My*

---

[119] "How Barack Proposed To Michelle Obama." 02:00. YouTube.
[120] "A Mother's Promise: Barack's Biography." 04:40. YouTube.

Father. The book became a bestseller when reissued in 2004.

In 1995, after a year of battling ovarian and uterine cancer, Barack's mother passed away. He writes in the preface of the reissuing of his book:

"I think sometimes that had I known she would not survive her illness, I might have written a different book, less a meditation on the absent parent, more a celebration
of the one who was the single constant in my life."
Barack Obama[121]

He and his mother were extremely close. The kindness and empathy that she had in her heart, he now has in his. This is evident through the philanthropic work they both pursued throughout their lives.

"I know that she was the kindest, most generous spirit I have ever known, and that what is best in me I owe to her."
Barack Obama[122]

♦

[121] Scott. "A Free-Spirited Wanderer Who Set Obama's Path." The New York Times.
[122] Scott. "A Free-Spirited Wanderer Who Set Obama's Path." The New York Times.

In Michelle's memoir *Becoming*, which became a #1 New York Times Bestseller, she recounts the difficulties the Obamas had with pregnancy early on

> *"It turns out that even two committed go-getters with a deep love and a robust work ethic can't will themselves into being pregnant."*
> *From Michelle Obama's memoir, Becoming*[123]

They had difficulty getting pregnant and sadly when Michelle finally did get pregnant, she had a miscarriage weeks later.

> *"I felt lost and alone and I felt like I failed because I didn't know how common miscarriages were because we don't talk about them. We sit in our own pain thinking that somehow, we're broken."*
> *Michelle Obama*[124]

The Obamas have been open about the use of infertility treatments and how those treatments assisted in their future pregnancies.

---

[123] "Michelle Obama opens up about miscarriage, IVF and marriage counseling: Part 2." 04:55. YouTube.
[124] "Michelle Obama opens up about miscarriage, IVF and marriage counseling: Part 2." 05:10. YouTube.

The Obamas had their first child, Malia Ann Obama, on July 4th, 1998. Her sister, Natasha Obama, a.k.a Sasha, would be born a few years later on July 10th, 2001.

Michelle also reveals in her book some of the difficulties she and Barack have faced within their own marriage, even seeking out counseling at one point, which she speaks about very favorably.

"I know too many young couples who struggle, and think that somehow there's something wrong with them, and I want them to know that Michelle and Barack Obama, who have a phenomenal marriage, and who love each other – we work on our marriage, and we get help with our marriage when we need it."
Michelle Obama[125]

In 1996 Barack Obama served his first two-year term as Illinois State Senator. He was re-elected in 1998, serving a four-year term and was re-elected a final term in 2002 where he served for another four-years.

Barack openly supported John Kerry and in 2004 was asked to deliver the keynote speech at the Democratic National Convention in support of Kerry. This speech put Barack Obama on the map and made him a household name. It was the first of many powerful

---

[125] Michelle Obama opens up about miscarriage, IVF and marriage counseling: Part 2." 06:25. YouTube.

speeches Barack would make that would help pave the way to the Oval Office.

"Tonight, is a particular honor for me because, let's face it, my presence on this stage is pretty unlikely."
Barack Obama at the Democratic National Convention, 2004[126]

On February 10th, 2007, Barack would make an announcement in Springfield, Illinois, in front of seventeen thousand people, declaring his candidacy for President of the United States. It was in this very location that Abraham Lincoln delivered his "House Divided," speech, in front of the Old State Capitol building.

"You read about some injustice, and you say, 'that's not right, somebody should fix that.' You realize nobody else is going to fix it if you don't."
Barack Obama[127]

Barack and Michelle worked hard on the campaign trail, spreading messages of hope and change that resonated with people, young and old, from all races and creeds. He received support from celebrities such as Beyoncé, Jay-Z, Jennifer Lopez, Leonardo DiCaprio, Morgan

---

[126] "Obama's 2004 DNC keynote speech." 00:05. YouTube.
[127] "A Mother's Promise: Barack's Biography." 05:05. YouTube.

Freeman, Maya Angelou, Aretha Franklin, Barbra Streisand, and Oprah Winfrey to list a few.

Oprah was such a strong supporter of Barack's that she even accompanied him on the campaign trail while visiting key states like Iowa, New Hampshire, and South Carolina.

On August 28th, 2008, Barack Obama made his acceptance speech after receiving the Democratic nomination for president of the United States. Martin Luther King Jr. made his infamous I Have a Dream speech[128] on this very same date.

"I was never the likeliest candidate for this office. We didn't start with much money or many endorsements. Our campaign was not hatched in the halls of Washington — it began in the backyards of Des Moines and the living rooms of Concord and the front porches of Charleston."

Barack Obama[129]

Barack Obama became the 44th President of the United States and the first African American President of the United States.

---

128 "'I Have A Dream' Speech, In Its Entirety." 2010. NPR.

129 "Barack Obama's 2008 acceptance speech." 06:10. YouTube.

"If you're disappointed by your elected officials, grab a clipboard, get some signatures, and run for office yourself."
Barack Obama[130]

"Obama received the largest share of the popular vote won by a Democrat since Lyndon B. Johnson in 1964 and was the first Democrat to win an outright majority of the popular vote since Jimmy Carter in 1976."[131]

"Our time has come, our movement is real, and change is coming to America."
Barack Obama[132]

Change did come. Barack Obama took office in 2009 and was re-elected in 2012. His Inauguration Day even fell on Martin Luther King Jr. Day, one of his biggest idols along with Abraham Lincoln.

Before Barack stepped into office, the country was on the brink of a major economic depression, and America was involved in two wars. One in Afghanistan and one in Iraq.

---

[130] "Barack Obama's final speech as president" 01:56. YouTube.
[131] "2008 United States presidential election." Wikipedia.
[132] "Obama's Roots Lie In A Humble Kenyan Village." 00:02. YouTube.

*"We know the battle ahead will be long,
but always remember that no matter what obstacles
stand in our way, nothing can stand in the way of the
power of millions of voices calling for change."*
Barack Obama[133]

By the time Obama left office he had ended the war in Iraq, bringing home over 100,000 troops. He made great strides in Afghanistan, bringing over 90,000 out of 100,000 troops home as well.
He created 14 million jobs for the American people, cut deficits by almost three-quarters, and avoided a major economic crisis.

Barack Obama provided bailout funding for the auto industry, saving 1.5 million jobs. The auto industry was in decline when Obama took office. The bailout revitalized the industry, and it was then seeing its best job growth since the 1990s.

*"Every single day I wake up and I have the possibility,
the opportunity, of making things a little bit
better for somebody out there."*
*Barack Obama when asked, "If he's happy,"
while he was still in office.[134]*

One of the most well-known accomplishments of Barack Obama's time in office was the Affordable Care Act, also

---

[133] "Yes We Can - Barack Obama Music Video." 01:55. YouTube.
[134] "Guy Asks Obama If He Is Happy." 02:20. YouTube.

known as Obamacare. This revolutionized the healthcare industry and provided health care to over 20 million Americans. Under the Affordable Care Act 9/10 Americans were insured.

Obamacare protected as many as 129 million adults and up to 19 million children with pre-existing conditions, who would have normally been unable to receive affordable care.

During Barack Obama's time in office, he restored relations with Cuba and signed the National Defense Authorization Act banning torture, rolling back torture policies from the previous administration led by George W. Bush.

Barack Obama signed an executive order prohibiting discrimination in the workplace for LGBT (lesbian, gay, bisexual and transgender) individuals. He legalized same-sex marriage country-wide and repealed, "Don't ask, don't tell."

"Don't ask, don't tell," prohibited people who were openly gay, lesbian or bisexual from serving in the United States military. Under Obama, LGBT individuals were able to be open about who they were while serving in the U.S. military.

"In April of 2014, President Obama signed an Executive Order to prevent workplace discrimination and empower workers to take control over negotiations regarding their pay. In addition, he signed a Presidential Memorandum directing the Secretary of Labor to require federal contractors to submit data on employee compensation by race and gender, helping employers take proactive efforts to ensure fair pay for their employees."[135]

In 2010 President Obama signed the Dodd-Frank Wall Street Reform and Consumer Protection Act into law. Multiple organizations were created to protect consumers, increase safety standards, and monitor the risk factors of major financial institutions.

These reform measures were in large part made into law to help prevent the same type of financial crisis that was seen in 2008 from happening again. Barack Obama even made credit card reforms through the Credit Card Accountability, Responsibility, and Disclosure (CARD) Act of 2009.

This act ended the days of credit card companies sending out confusing contracts and then locking consumers into long-term contracts with soaring interest rates they might not have been aware of.

Because of this act, credit card companies were required to make sure that contracts were written in plain English. The act strengthened the protection consumers had when dealing with credit card companies and also increased the penalties of those individuals who partook in deceptive practices.

---

[135] "Understand the Basics." Obama White House Archives.

President Obama made great strides to reduce our reliance on foreign oil while also protecting the environment.

"In total, the Administration's national program to improve fuel economy and reduce greenhouse gas emissions will save consumers more than $1.7 trillion at the gas pump and reduce U.S. oil consumption by 12 billion barrels."[136]

The goal was to, "...increase fuel economy to the equivalent of 54.5 mpg for cars and light-duty trucks by Model Year 2025."[137]

He also created the Clean Power Plan. The Clean Power Plan rewarded states that set energy efficiency targets for themselves while setting the target of reducing carbon pollution by power plants by 32% by 2030.

"A lot of power companies have already begun modernizing their plants, reducing their emissions and, by the way, creating new jobs in the process. Nearly a dozen states have already set up their own market-based programs to reduce carbon pollution. About half of our States have set energy efficiency targets. More than 35 have set renewable energy targets.

Over a thousand mayors have signed an agreement to cut carbon pollution in their cities. And last

[136] "Obama Administration Finalizes Historic 54.5 MPG Fuel Efficiency Standards." Obama White House Archives.

[137] "Obama Administration Finalizes Historic 54.5 MPG Fuel Efficiency Standards." Obama White House Archives.

week, 13 of our biggest companies, including UPS and Walmart and GM, made bold, new commitments to cut their emissions and deploy more clean energy."[138]

Barack Obama, has been recognized by the Wilderness Hall of Fame for his accomplishments as protecting, "...more lands, waters and cultural sites than any other president..."[139]

President Obama improved education by replacing the previous Bush administrations' "No Child Left Behind" with "Race to the Top". "No Child Left Behind" increased Federal spending without seeing improvements in education for students. "Race to the Top" created better assessments and provided more information to schools and parents regarding their children's progress. "Race to the Top," also provided additional support & resources for teachers. As a result, high school graduation rates hit new records, increasing over 80% under the Obama Administration.

◆

Michelle Obama led and participated in many initiatives during her and Barack's time in the White House.

---

[138] "Remarks Announcing the Environmental Protection Agency's Clean Power Plan." The American Presidency Project.

[139] "The Wilderness Hall of Fame: 13 presidents who were true conservation leaders." The Wilderness Society.

"Michelle LaVaughn Robinson, girl of the South Side, for the past 25 years you have not only been my wife and mother of my children, you have been my best friend. You took on a role you didn't ask for and you made it your own with grace and with grit and with style and with humor."
Barack Obama[140]

Michelle and Dr. Jill Biden launched, "Joining Forces." The purpose of which was to provide veterans, members of service and their families with education, wellness, mental health and employment opportunities across the United States.

"The thing we've learned as we've watched this campaign is that people, women, are capable of doing more than one thing well at the same time and I've had to juggle being mom-in-chief and having a career for a long time."
Michelle Obama[141]

Michelle launched "Reach Higher," which focused on encouraging continuing education for students after high school and, "Let Girls Learn," whose main purpose was

---

[140] "Obama tears up while speaking about wife, daughters during farewell speech." 00:42. YouTube.
[141] "60 Minutes, 11.16.08." 33:10. YouTube. https://www.youtube.com/watch?v=_6TmlwNYojU.

to provide more educational opportunities for young women.

She also launched, "Let's Move," in 2010 with the goal of improving health in children and families.

"...watching Michelle as first lady has just increased my awe and respect for her."
Barack Obama[142]

"Because of our collective efforts to raise a healthier generation, 1 in 4 Americans now live in a community where their local elected official has committed to creating a healthier environment. Fifty million kids have more nutritious school meals and snacks. Thousands of chain restaurants now offer healthier options on kids' menus..."[143]

Even nutrition fact labels improved because of, "Let's Move." "The final label requires Added Sugars to be declared to help consumers know how much sugar is added to the product during the processing of foods. The label features a revamped format that highlights key information, such as calories and servings per container.

---

[142] "The Final Interview With The Obamas | People." 14:05. YouTube.
[143] "What the changes might look like through the eyes of a child: #LetsMove." 01:53. Facebook.

It also replaces out-of-date serving sizes to better align with the amount consumers actually eat."[144]

Michelle and Barack worked hard to create a culture of inclusion during their time in the White House. African dance classes were held at the White House in honor of Black History Month.
The Obamas hosted sleepover events and had a Girl Scout camping night where 50 girl scouts from across the U.S. were invited to camp out on the White House lawn overnight. They even started the first White House Science Fair.

The work that both Barack and Michelle put into their time in office was nothing short of spectacular. They united individuals of all backgrounds under one shared belief: that people could create positive change in the world and were capable of extraordinary things.

[144] Eschmeyer. "Announcing The Modernized Nutrition Facts Label." Let's Move!

"...He has been a role model to millions of people from all backgrounds and no one can dispute that. I don't care what party you belong to. When you think of father, when you think of a good husband, somebody with strong values - All the things that people say they admire most in people and want in a leader, Barack Obama has been that and more."
Michelle Obama[145]

◆

With all of these accomplishments, it's hard to believe that Barack came from such a modest background, but he did. He climbed his way to the top, a pinnacle reached by only 43 other individuals in history.

Barack's origin story, combined with him becoming the 44th President of the United States and the first to be African American, serves as an inspiration to us all. He was, and continues to be, a trailblazer, encouraging people of all genders, ages, and ethnicities that you can create change.

You can be the person you've always wanted to be. You don't have to be born with a silver spoon, you just need to believe in yourself and keep pushing forward, even in times of strife —yes, we can.

---

[145] "The Final Interview With The Obamas | People." 25:20. YouTube.

"What I want is people to once again feel like
'If I'm out there working hard and doing the right thing,
opportunity's right there for me to grab.' And I think it
is...I want everybody to feel in their own lives day to day
that
opportunity is right there in front of them."
Barack Obama, when asked by Oprah,
"What do you want your legacy to be?"[146]

Chain of Events

Barack Obama was born in Honolulu, Hawaii on August 4th, 1961. He was raised by a single mom and his grandparents between Hawaii and Indonesia in his youth. Education was important to both Barack and his mother.

His mother, Ann instilled those values into him, and he followed through, going on to attend Occidental College in Los Angeles, California and Columbia University in New York City, NY.

When he graduated from Columbia University, Barack was offered a job in Chicago working as a community organizer.

He went back to school, this time to Harvard Law School, where he would meet his future wife, Michelle. Barack enrolled in a summer program at a law firm in

---

[146] Oprah, President Obama And First Lady Michelle Obama." 33:45. YouTube.

Chicago where Michelle was working at the time. She would be his mentor, and after a month of getting to know each other, they went on their first date.

Barack graduated *magna cum laude* from Harvard Law School in 1991 and married Michelle on October 3rd, 1992. His first book, *Dreams from My Father* was published in 1995.

Between 1997-2004 he would serve as Illinois State Senator. In 2004 he delivered the keynote speech at the Democratic National Convention, this speech put Barack on the map making him a household name.

In 2007 Barack announced that he would be running for President of the United States and in 2008 he became the 44th president and the first African American President of the United States of America. Barack was re-elected in 2012 and remains active in politics to this day.

End of Chapter Exercises

o Whose success story were you most surprised to learn about and why?

_____

_____

_____

o Research three people who came from similar backgrounds as you and accomplished the same/similar goals that you are in pursuit of. Name those individuals below:

_____

_____

_____

o   Name some commonalities between those three
    individuals' success stories. For example, did they
    perform similar actions to each other or study the
    same subjects? How did they place themselves in
    situations that helped them accomplish their
    goals?

_____

_____

_____

o   What advice or quotes can you find from those
    who have achieved the same/similar goals to the
    ones you're pursuing? List them below:

_____

_____

_____

o What actions would you now like to take after
   learning the origin stories of people who have
   accomplished the same or similar goals?

_____

_____

_____

o What advice would you give someone who is
   actively pursuing the same or similar goals that
   you are?

_____

_____

_____

o Write your own success story from the future:

For example, what might your own "chain of events" look like after accomplishing your goal?
✧ *Include your background, where you are in your journey, and where you see yourself in 1, 5 or 10 years.*

_____

_____

_____

Pass It On

The final section of *Motion* is Pass It On. Now that you're almost at the finish line, help others as they travel on their own paths towards success.

We've all experienced the negativity coming from within us and also coming from those around us — from people who we've always looked up to and admired. It's heartbreaking to hear words of discouragement from people we respect and love.

But, as discouraging as it is to hear, "You won't be able to...You won't succeed," it's even more powerful to hear, "I believe in you and know you can!"

Being the voice that you wish you had heard on your own journey can quite literally change the course of a person's life, forever. The number one hurdle we all have to get over is belief, before anything else. And that's not magic, it's fact.

Before we do anything, we think about it. From small things like getting up and walking to the store to more significant undertakings like going to school and getting a degree.

If we didn't think we could,
we wouldn't even try.

This applies to all thoughts, large and small. You have to believe you can achieve your dreams with such certainty that no person or event will be able to convince you otherwise.

Although it could be one of the most challenging barriers to breakthrough, it's possible to achieve it through a shift in your line of thinking.

A main focal point of the previous section was the success of others who had modest upbringings yet overcame challenges in their lives, allowing them to reach their dreams.

If there are other people out there who have become wildly successful yet started from point A as most people do, why can't we? Why can't we succeed? Why can't we reach our goals and our dreams?

By encouraging others to reach their full potential, you're joining them on their path towards success. You can be the one force in someone's life that they will remember and be grateful for. The one voice of reason that was able to prove to them that they *could* succeed, because someone other than themselves believed it was possible.

That extra support helps; even though it isn't necessary, it's welcomed and can produce spectacular results, resonating with people for years to come. With the proper guidance and support, I believe *everyone* has the ability to succeed. Which, of course, means achieving their own individual definition of success.

You have the power to change history
by encouraging others to pursue their dreams.

The more people who believe they can, the more we can do as a society and as a species. We'd have more painters and artists, more photographers and actors. We'd have more teachers and firefighters and more people continuing their education.

Remember when you were a kid and were asked what you wanted to be when you grew up? Maybe it was a ballerina or a scientist or an astronaut or a veterinarian. So why and when did that belief change? Your interests might have changed, and that's fine, but if you became discouraged at some point instead, then get back on track and help others do the same.

How can you recognize when someone is in need of guidance? It can be hard to see, but there are some tell-tale signs. The first is that they're generally unhappy.

They could be unhappy for so many reasons. Problems in their personal lives, at home, at school, or maybe they're just in a rut. Unhappiness can stem from many different sources; the first step is establishing the root of the problem. Have a talk with the person and establish what's really at the source of their discontent.

If it's because they don't have time, figure out what they're wanting to spend their time on. Then establish what things they can do that would give them more time in their day. For the most part, people won't just come to you and say, "I need help," but that doesn't mean that your help isn't needed or wanted.

Start by trying to connect by establishing the causes of their dissatisfaction. Work with them on figuring out things they can do in the short term and the long term that will bring them to their goals.

There is satisfaction in the pursuit of one's goals, as well as in the achieving of them.

Knowing that you're on the right path is half the battle.

Be sure to be encouraging and make the individual aware of real people who were just like them at one point and have achieved similar goals. It's important to note that you don't want to shift someone's focus towards a goal that *you believe* would be more suitable for them.

As long as their goals keep themselves and the people around them safe and happy, then they have to be allowed and encouraged to pursue them.
We have to remove our own biases and opinions and be a neutral party whose sole purpose is to support and encourage, not sway, based on what we feel "would be best".

How do you help others who feel they aren't capable of succeeding? You have to remember, that you're potentially pushing against years of discouragement. Maybe the person you're trying to help grew up surrounded by people telling them only *other* people can achieve great things, and they're not one of them.

Sadly, this is a very familiar scenario. However, knowing that allows us to shift those thoughts out of the negative and into the positive.
Make it real.

You've been through *Motion*; you know the steps you need to take in order to create a very clear path to success. Show them that path. Work them through each step they'll need to take in order to achieve their goals.

From the very first step of believing they can, to the final step of accepting their first Oscar or saving their first life as a paramedic, whatever their goal is, show them the way, show them the path, show them it's possible.

If we just have a dream and no clear path on how to attain it, then it's going to live above us — unattainable, inaccessible and always out of reach.

It's about each step on that path. It doesn't matter how high the staircase may be, each step will bring them closer and closer to their dreams and the belief they have in themselves will continue to grow over time.

If someone doesn't think they can accomplish a major goal, show them all the smaller goals they can achieve first. Those are achievable accomplishments that will instill a stronger faith in themselves and the belief that maybe their dreams are more attainable than they realized.

What do you do when someone has started working towards achieving their goals, but has "failed?" The illusion of failure is probably the falsity I have the biggest problem with.

Failure only exists when you stop trying.
Everything before that is education.

You may stumble or experience a roadblock, but as long as you learn from that event, you can't fail! The only way you can fail is if you stop right there and never try again.

When you're at your lowest and start thinking, "Nothing I've done has worked so far; maybe I really won't be successful," remember, these are the lies we are telling ourselves because we're feeling run down, tired and dejected.

Fine, feel that way for a moment and allow others to feel it too, but when the wallowing is over, get up and get back to work!

Help others on their own journeys. Few things are more needed and rewarding.

Bibliography

AACTA. n.d. "Winners & Nominees I 5th AACTA Awards." *Winners & Nominees I AACTA.* Accessed December 7, 2021. https://www.aacta.org/aacta-awards/past-awards/5th-aacta-awards/.

ABC News. 2018. "Michelle Obama opens up about miscarriage, IVF and marriage counseling: Part 2." *YouTube.* 12 11. https://www.youtube.com/watch?v=zDBb88MOYuQ&t=330s.

2021. "Accepts Nominations for 2021 National Medal of Arts I National Endowment for the Arts." *National Endowment for the Arts.* February 12. Accessed December 8, 2021. https://www.arts.gov/about/news/2021/national-endowment-arts-accepts-nominations-2021-national-medal-arts.

American Sleep Association. n.d. "Sleep Statistics: Data About Sleep Disorders." Accessed December 7, 2021. https://www.sleepassociation.org/about-sleep/sleep-statistics/.

Arts & Sciences Web Team. 2015. "Barack Obama's Mother ... and the UW Department of Anthropology I Department of Anthropology I University of Washington." *Anthropology I University of Washington.* April 1. Accessed December 7, 2021. https://anthropology.washington.edu/news/2015/04/01/barack-obamas-mother-and-uw-department-anthropology.

Audio Publishers Association. 2020. "2020 AUDIE
AWARDS TO HONOR STEPHEN KING FOR
LIFETIME ACHIEVEMENT Bestselling authors
Emma Straub, Adam Silvera, and Elle colum."
Audio Publishers Association. January 8.
Accessed December 7, 2021.
https://www.audiopub.org/uploads/pdf/King-and-
judges-announcement.pdf.

BAFTA. n.d. "BAFTA Awards Search I BAFTA Awards."
BAFTA Awards Search I BAFTA Awards.
Accessed December 7, 2021.
http://awards.bafta.org/keyword-
search?keywords=%22Kate%20Winslet%22.

BAFTA Guru. 2016. "Kate Winslet: A Life In Pictures."
YouTube. September 9. Accessed December 8,
2021.
https://www.youtube.com/watch?v=1aP96Q9Vkwl.

BAILEY, ALYSSA. 2016. "Kate Winslet BAFTA Speech -
Kate Winslet on Self Doubt." *ELLE.* February 16.
Accessed December 7, 2021.
https://www.elle.com/culture/celebrities/news/a341
17/kate-winslet-bafta-backstage-speech/.

BarackObamadotcom. 2008. "A Mother's Promise:
Barack's Biography." *YouTube.* October 3.
Accessed December 8, 2021.
https://www.youtube.com/watch?v=OjF51ALu0sc.

—. 2008. "American Stories, American Solutions: 30
Minute Special." *YouTube.* October 29. Accessed
December 8, 2021.
https://www.youtube.com/watch?v=GtREqAmLso
A.

BBC Studios. 2009. "Carrie: Rescued from the Bin I Mark Lawson Talks to Stephen King I BBC Studios." *YouTube*. June 5. Accessed December 8, 2021. https://www.youtube.com/watch?v=xgqj7dbLSas.

Bender, Paula. 2009. "Legacy of the President's Mother: UH alumna Ann Dunham built bridges and bettered lives I Malamalama, The Magazine of the University of Hawai'i System." *University of Hawaii System*. January 14. Accessed December 7, 2021. http://www.hawaii.edu/malamalama/2009/01/lessons-for-president-obama/.

BIFA. 2015. "Kate Winslet to receive The Variety Award · BIFA · British Independent Film Awards." *British Independent Film Awards*. October 27. Accessed December 9, 2021. https://www.bifa.film/news/kate-winslet-to-receive-the-variety-award/.

Bobblehead Conan. 2017. "Conan O'Brien 'Kate Winslet 3/18/04." *YouTube*. February 16. Accessed December 8, 2021. https://www.youtube.com/watch?v=B9WIp-B1DcM.

n.d. "Category List – The Grand Master I Edgars Database." *The Edgar Awards*. Accessed December 7, 2021. http://theedgars.com/awards/category-list-the-grand-master/.

CBC Arts. 2007. "Booksellers honour 'heavy metal' King of writing." *CBC*. June 9. Accessed December 7, 2021.

https://www.cbc.ca/news/entertainment/bookseller
s-honour-heavy-metal-king-of-writing-1.672018.

CBS News. 2010. "60 Minutes, 11.16.08." *YouTube.*
November 4. Accessed December 9, 2021.
https://www.youtube.com/watch?v=_6TmlwNY0jU.

—. 2008. "The Obamas On Their Personal Transition."
CBS News. November 16. Accessed December 7,
2021. https://www.cbsnews.com/news/the-
obamas-on-their-personal-transition/.

CNN. 2016. "Obama's 2004 DNC keynote speech."
YouTube. July 27. Accessed December 8, 2021.
https://www.youtube.com/watch?v=ueMNqdB1QIE
.

—. 2012. "Raw Video: Barack Obama's 2008 acceptance
speech." *YouTube.* November 7. Accessed
December 8, 2021.
https://www.youtube.com/watch?v=LEo7lzfpdCU.

C-SPAN. 2009. "Pres. Obama National Address to
Students." *YouTube.* September 8. Accessed
December 8, 2021.
https://www.youtube.com/watch?v=3iqsxCWjCvl.

Dolan, Kerry A, and Jennifer Wang. 2021. "America's
Richest Self-Made Women 2021." *Forbes.* August
5. Accessed December 8, 2021.
https://www.forbes.com/self-made-women/.

Dolan, Kerry A, and Neil Jamieson. n.d. "Forbes
Billionaires 2021: The Richest People in the
World." *Forbes.* Accessed December 7, 2021.
https://www.forbes.com/billionaires/.

Donahue, Phil. 2010. "Oprah Winfrey - The 2010 TIME
100 - TIME." *Videos Index on TIME.com.* April 29.
Accessed December 7, 2021.

http://content.time.com/time/specials/packages/arti
cle/0,28804,1984685_1984940_1985540,00.html.

Edleson, Harriet. 2019. "More Americans Working or
Looking for Work After 65." *AARP*. April 22.
Accessed November 24, 2021.
https://www.aarp.org/work/employers/info-
2019/americans-working-past-65.html.

Eggers, Dave, and Barack Obama. 2010. "60 Minutes,
11.16.08." *YouTube*. November 4. Accessed
December 8, 2021.
https://www.youtube.com/watch?v=_6TmlwNY0jU.

Elder, MD, MPH, FACP, Charles, Sanford Nidich, EdD,
Francis Moriarty, EdD, and Randi Nidich, EdD.
2014. "Effect of transcendental meditation on
employee stress, depression, and burnout: a
randomized controlled study." *The Permanente
Journal* 18 (1): 19-23.
https://www.ncbi.nlm.nih.gov/pmc/articles/PMC39
51026/.

enjoyyourself23. 2012. "Kate Winslet's first Titanic screen
test." *YouTube*. September 8. Accessed
December 8, 2021.
https://www.youtube.com/watch?v=Jk-OZiiZs3o.

Eschmeyer, Debra. 2016. "Announcing The Modernized
Nutrition Facts Label I Let's." *Let's Move!* May 20.
Accessed December 7, 2021.
https://letsmove.obamawhitehouse.archives.gov/bl
og/2016/05/20/announcing-modernized-nutrition-
facts-label.

European Film Awards. n.d. "Titanic - Film." *European
Film Awards*. Accessed December 7, 2021.

https://www.europeanfilmawards.eu/en_EN/film/tit
anic.5495.

FIRST®. 2017. "FIRST Honors President Barack Obama,
Commits to Closing STEM Equity Gap I FIRST."
FIRST Inspires. November 8. Accessed
December 7, 2021.
https://www.firstinspires.org/about/press-
room/first-honors-president-barack-obama-
commits-to-closing-stem-equity-gap.

Forbes. 2021. "#12 Oprah Winfrey Entrepreneur,
Personality, Philanthropist." 11 04.
https://www.forbes.com/profile/oprah-
winfrey/?sh=55de400c5745.

GAR MED. 2018. "Oprah 2011 05 02 President Obama
And First Lady Michelle Obama." *YouTube.*
February 26. Accessed December 8, 2021.
https://www.youtube.com/watch?v=3N2oQ2s8uuE
.

Global News. 2017. "Obama tears up while speaking
about wife, daughters during farewell speech."
YouTube. January 11. Accessed December 8,
2021.
https://www.youtube.com/watch?v=25Y0HkX6J4c.

Greene, Andy. 2014. "Stephen King: The Rolling Stone
Interview." *Rolling Stone.* October 31. Accessed
December 7, 2021.
https://www.rollingstone.com/culture/culture-
features/stephen-king-the-rolling-stone-interview-
191529/.

Grossberg, Josh. 2014. "President Obama honored by
USC Shoah Foundation." *USC News.* May 8.
Accessed December 7, 2021.

https://news.usc.edu/62416/obama-honored-with-usc-shoah-foundations-ambassador-for-humanity-award/.

Guardian News. 2017. "Barack Obama's final speech as president – video highlights." *YouTube.* January 11. Accessed December 8, 2021. https://www.youtube.com/watch?v=k0jJL_YFyIU.

Harvard Law Review. n.d. "About the Harvard Law Review." *Harvard Law Review.* Accessed December 7, 2021. https://harvardlawreview.org/about/.

Heller, Karen. 2016. "Meet the writers who still sell millions of books. Actually, hundreds of millions." *The Washington Post.* December 20. Accessed November 24, 2021. https://www.washingtonpost.com/lifestyle/style/meet-the-elite-group-of-authors-who-sell-100-million-books-or-350-million/2016/12/20/db3c6a66-bb0f-11e6-94ac-3d324840106c_story.html.

Hollywood Walk of Fame. n.d. "Kate Winslet." *Hollywood Walk of Fame.* Accessed December 7, 2021. https://walkoffame.com/kate-winslet/.

IMDb. n.d. "Kate Winslet - Awards." *IMDb.* Accessed December 7, 2021. https://www.imdb.com/name/nm0000701/awards.

—. n.d. "Titanic (1997) - Awards." *IMDb.* Accessed December 7, 2021. https://www.imdb.com/title/tt0120338/awards.

Independent.ie. 2017. "Kate Winslet and Jodie Foster among winners at Women Of The Year Awards." *Independent.ie.* November 2. Accessed December 9, 2021.

https://www.independent.ie/style/celebrity/celebrity
-news/kate-winslet-and-jodie-foster-among-
winners-at-women-of-the-year-awards-
36285358.html.

Jackson, David. 2013. "Obama to receive special award
in Israel." *USA Today.* February 18. Accessed
December 7, 2021.
https://www.usatoday.com/story/theoval/2013/02/1
8/obama-award-israel-shimon-peres-benjamin-
netanyahu/1927927/.

n.d. "Jean Hersholt Humanitarian Award." *Oscars.org.*
Accessed December 8, 2021.
https://www.oscars.org/governors/hersholt.

Journeyman Pictures. 2016. "Obama's Roots Lie In A
Humble Kenyan Village (2008)." *YouTube.* June
29. Accessed December 8, 2021.
https://www.youtube.com/watch?v=CnLOV73pSic.

King, Tabitha. n.d. "The Author." *Stephen King.*
Accessed December 7, 2021.
https://stephenking.com/the-author/.

Lavelle Luthy. 2018. "Oprah Winfrey 1988 Barbara
Walters Interviews Of A Lifetime." *YouTube.*
January 28. Accessed December 8, 2021.
https://www.youtube.com/watch?v=NMbv9xtmDvl.

Let's Move. 2016. "After years of working together to
build a healthier America, see what the changes
might look like through the eyes of a child:
http://go.wh.gov/9quFMK #LetsMove." *Facebook.*
12 9.
https://www.facebook.com/letsmove/videos/10154
187975697759.

LinkedIn. n.d. *About LinkedIn.* Accessed November 24, 2021. https://about.linkedin.com/.

Luiggi-Hernandez, MPH, José G., Jean Woo, MD, Megan Hamm, PhD, Carol M. Greco, PhD, Debra K. Weiner, MD, and Natalie E. Morone, MD, MS. 2018. "Mindfulness for Chronic Low Back Pain: A Qualitative Analysis." *Pain Medicine* 19 (11): 2138–2145. https://academic.oup.com/painmedicine/article/19/11/2138/4083474?login=true.

Manufacturing Intellect. 2017. "Young Oprah Winfrey interview on her Life and Career (1991)." *YouTube.* August 27. Accessed December 8, 2021. https://www.youtube.com/watch?v=1ObDKKW-sn8.

Michael McIntee. 2014. "Guy Asks Obama If He Is Happy. Watch What He Says." *YouTube.* February 1. Accessed December 8, 2021. https://www.youtube.com/watch?v=SAxKJC0Elds.

Momentum-Aholic. 2017. "Stephen King reveals the secret to his success." *YouTube.* August 30. Accessed December 8, 2021. https://www.youtube.com/watch?v=vs07oC_33sY.

MPR News. 2009. "Talking Volumes: Stephen King on "Carrie"." *YouTube.* November 19. Accessed December 8, 2021. https://www.youtube.com/watch?v=agGuYCmJllw.

NAACP Image Awards. 2010. "Sen. Barack Obama - 36th NAACP Image Awards - Chairman's Award." *YouTube.* October 30. Accessed December 8, 2021.

https://www.youtube.com/watch?v=Zona7DqcKYA
.

Nasaw, Daniel. 2008. "Obama pauses campaign to visit ailing grandmother | US elections 2008." *The Guardian.* October 21. Accessed December 7, 2021. https://www.theguardian.com/world/2008/oct/21/barack-obama-campaign-grandmother-illness.

National Book Foundation. n.d. "Stephen King Accepts the 2003 Medal for Distinguished Contribution to American Letters - National Book Foundation." *National Book Award.* Accessed December 7, 2021. https://www.nationalbook.org/stephen-king-accepts-the-2003-medal-for-distinguished-contribution-to-american-letters/.

National Endowment for the Arts. n.d. "Stephen King." *National Endowment for the Arts.* Accessed December 7, 2021. https://www.arts.gov/honors/medals/stephen-king.

NME. 2009. "Shockwaves NME Awards 2009: The Winners." *NME.* February 26. Accessed December 9, 2021. https://www.nme.com/news/music/shockwaves-nme-awards-2008-big-gig-8-1304431.

Nobel Prize. 2009. "2009 Nobel Peace Prize Lecture by Barack Obama." *Youtube.* 12 17. https://www.youtube.com/watch?v=AORo-YEXxNQ&list=PL_A0XHYv91aGyiLgPdxsl3woA_OoPiSWy&index=6&t=0s.

Nobel Prize organisation. n.d. "The Nobel Peace Prize for 2009 to President Barack Obama - Press release - NobelPrize.org." *Nobel Prize.* Accessed

December 7, 2021.
https://www.nobelprize.org/prizes/peace/2009/pre
ss-release/.

NPR. 2010. "'I Have A Dream' Speech, In Its Entirety."
NPR. January 18. Accessed December 7, 2021.
https://www.npr.org/2010/01/18/122701268/i-
have-a-dream-speech-in-its-entirety.

2012. "Obama Administration Finalizes Historic 54.5
MPG Fuel Efficiency Standards." *Obama White
House Archives.* August 28. Accessed December
7, 2021.
https://obamawhitehouse.archives.gov/the-press-
office/2012/08/28/obama-administration-finalizes-
historic-545-MPG-fuel-efficiency-standard.

Obama, Barack. n.d. "Barack and Michelle Obama's First
Date - Famous Firsts." *Oprah.com.* Accessed
December 7, 2021.
http://www.oprah.com/world/barack-and-michelle-
obamas-first-date-famous-firsts.

Official Charts. n.d. "KATE WINSLET I full Official Chart
History." *Official Charts.* Accessed December 7,
2021.
https://www.officialcharts.com/artist/5972/kate-
winslet/.

Ong, PhD, Jason C., Rachel Manber, PhD, Zindel Segal,
PhD, Yinglin Xia, PhD, Shauna Shapiro, PhD, and
James K. Wyatt, PhD. 2014. "A randomized
controlled trial of mindfulness meditation for
chronic insomnia." *Sleep* 37 (9): 1553–1563.
https://www.ncbi.nlm.nih.gov/pmc/articles/PMC41
53063/.

2004. "Online Extra: A Talk with Oprah Winfrey."
   Bloomberg.com. November 28. Accessed
   December 7, 2021.
   https://www.bloomberg.com/news/articles/2004-
   11-28/online-extra-a-talk-with-oprah-winfrey.
2011. "Oprah to receive humanitarian award." *CBS
   News*. November 8. Accessed December 7, 2021.
   https://www.cbsnews.com/news/oprah-to-receive-
   humanitarian-award/.
Oscars. 2009. "Kate Winslet winning Best Actress for
   "The Reader." *YouTube*. 2 25.
   https://www.youtube.com/watch?v=PxzQSWx9IGs
   &list=PLQixgkecC3PkTdZgiiL7GUa_GZqZdLvMp
   &index=284.
—. 2011. "Oprah Winfrey accepts her Jean Hersholt
   Humanitarian Award at the 2011 Governors
   Awards." *YouTube*. November 14. Accessed
   December 8, 2021.
   https://www.youtube.com/watch?v=zGWLw_E8IM
   0.
Parko77. 2010. "Stephen King Interview - The Today
   Show (1999)." *YouTube*. February 4. Accessed
   December 8, 2021.
   https://www.youtube.com/watch?v=CHNUhIc9Fig.
People. 2016. "The Final Interview With The Obamas
   (Full Interview) I PEN I People." *YouTube*. 12 20.
   https://www.youtube.com/watch?v=iH1ZJVqJO3Y
   &t=2s.
Proudfoot, Judith G., Philip J. Corr, David E. Guest, and
   Graham Dunn. 2009. "Cognitive-behavioural
   training to change attributional style improves
   employee well-being, job satisfaction, productivity,

and turnover." *Elsevier* n.d.: 147-153.
https://iveronicawalsh.files.wordpress.com/2014/0
4/cbtrainingreport.pdf.

2018. "Read Oprah Winfrey's rousing Golden Globes speech." *CNN.* January 10. Accessed December 7, 2021.
https://www.cnn.com/2018/01/08/entertainment/op
rah-globes-speech-transcript/index.html.

Recording Academy. n.d. "Barack Obama I Artist." *GRAMMY.com.* Accessed December 7, 2021.
https://www.grammy.com/grammys/artists/barack-
obama/4975.

—. n.d. "Kate Winslet I Artist." *GRAMMY.com.* Accessed December 7, 2021.
https://www.grammy.com/grammys/artists/kate-
winslet/15699.

Sampson, Hannah. 2019. "What does America have against vacation?" *The Washington Post.* August 28. Accessed November 24, 2021.
https://www.washingtonpost.com/travel/2019/08/2
8/what-does-america-have-against-vacation/.

Samuels, David. 2008. "Barack Obama, The Invisible Man." *CBS News.* October 8. Accessed December 7, 2021. https://www.cbsnews.com/news/barack-
obama-the-invisible-man/.

Schnell, Lindsay. 2020. "Women of Century Arts, Literature and Media: Oprah on USA TODAY list." *USA Today.* August 13. Accessed December 7, 2021. https://www.usatoday.com/in-
depth/life/women-of-the-
century/2020/08/13/media-arts-literature-woman-
history-oprah-author/5474772002/.

SCORE. n.d. *SCORE: Homepage.* Accessed November 24, 2021. https://www.score.org/.

Scott, Janny. 2008. "A Free-Spirited Wanderer Who Set Obama's Path (Published 2008)." *The New York Times.* March 14. Accessed December 7, 2021. https://www.nytimes.com/2008/03/14/us/politics/14obama.html?pagewanted=all.

Screen Actors Guild Awards. 2015. "Nominations Announced for the 22nd Annual Screen Actors Guild Awards." *Screen Actors Guild Awards.* December 9. Accessed December 7, 2021. https://www.sagawards.org/media/news/releases/nominations-announced-22nd-annual-screen-actors-guild-awards.

Simply Speech. 2017. "Hollywood actress Kate Winslet's speech on overcoming bullies at WE Day." *YouTube.* March 27. Accessed December 8, 2021. https://www.youtube.com/watch?v=D8JQRENH09I.

Stevens, Lance, and Lawrence Mallory. 2019. "US Seniors Pay Billions, yet Many Cannot Afford Healthcare." *Gallup News.* April 15. Accessed November 24, 2021. https://news.gallup.com/opinion/gallup/248741/seniors-pay-billions-yet-cannot-afford-healthcare.aspx.

Television Academy. n.d. "Kate Winslet - Emmy Awards, Nominations and Wins." *Television Academy.* Accessed December 7, 2021. https://www.emmys.com/bios/kate-winslet.

—. n.d. "Oprah Winfrey - Emmy Awards, Nominations and Wins." *Television Academy.* Accessed December 8, 2021. https://www.emmys.com/bios/oprah-winfrey.

—. 2015. "Oprah Winfrey accepts the Bob Hope Humanitarian Award." *Television Academy.* October 19. Accessed December 7, 2021. https://www.emmys.com/video/oprah-winfrey-accepts-bob-hope-humanitarian-award.

—. n.d. "Oprah Winfrey Hall of Fame Induction 1994." *Television Academy.* Accessed December 8, 2021. https://www.emmys.com/video/oprah-winfrey-hall-fame-induction-1994.

The Academy of Motion Picture Arts and Sciences. 2009. "Kate Winslet Academy Awards Acceptance Speech." *Oscar speech database.* February 22. Accessed December 7, 2021. http://aaopeechesdb.oscars.org/link/081-3/.

The Alumni Association. n.d. "Alumni Career Award." *UMaine Alumni Association.* Accessed December 7, 2021. https://www.umainealumni.com/alumni-career-award/.

The American Presidency Project. 2015. "Remarks Announcing the Environmental Protection Agency's Clean Power Plan | The American Presidency Project." *The American Presidency Project.* August 3. Accessed December 7, 2021. https://www.presidency.ucsb.edu/documents/remarks-announcing-the-environmental-protection-agencys-clean-power-plan.

The Hollywood Foreign Press Association. n.d. "Kate Winslet." *Golden Globes.* Accessed December 7,

2021. https://www.goldenglobes.com/person/kate-winslet.

The Horror Writers Association. n.d. "Lifetime Achievement Award." *Horror Writers Association.* Accessed December 7, 2021. https://horror.org/awards/laawd.htm.

The John F. Kennedy Presidential Library and Museum. 2017. "President Barack Obama Receives 2017 Centennial John F. Kennedy Profile in Courage Award." *JFK Library.* May 7. Accessed December 7, 2021. https://www.jfklibrary.org/about-us/news-and-press/press-releases/2017-profile-in-courage-award-ceremony.

The Late Show with Stephen Colbert. 2018. "How Barack Proposed To Michelle Obama." *YouTube.* 12 1. https://www.youtube.com/watch?v=PRhZCqAUwsc&t=95s.

—. 2017. "Kate Winslet Dropped Out Of School At 16." *YouTube.* December 1. Accessed December 9, 2021. https://www.youtube.com/watch?v=rT1N_urzERg.

The New York Times. 2013. "Obama Awards Presidential Medal of Freedom to Bill Clinton, 15 Others | The New York Times." *YouTube.* November 20. Accessed December 8, 2021. https://www.youtube.com/watch?v=eCnC4qQM9WA.

n.d. "The Wilderness Hall of Fame: 13 presidents who were true conservation leaders." *The Wilderness Society.* Accessed December 7, 2021. https://www.wilderness.org/articles/article/wilderne

ss-hall-fame-13-presidents-who-were-true-conservation-leaders#.

The Wilderness Society. n.d. "The Wilderness Hall of Fame: 13 presidents who were true conservation leaders." *The Wilderness Society.* Accessed December 7, 2021. https://www.wilderness.org/articles/article/wilderness-hall-fame-13-presidents-who-were-true-conservation-leaders#.

U.S. Department of Defense. n.d. "THE UNITED STATES OF AMERICA." *Department of Defense.* Accessed December 7, 2021. https://dod.defense.gov/Portals/1/Documents/pubs/POTUS_AWARD_CITATION.PDF.

n.d. "Understand the Basics." *Obama White House Archives.* Accessed December 7, 2021. https://obamawhitehouse.archives.gov/issues/equal-pay#top.

WeCan08. 2008. "Yes We Can - Barack Obama Music Video." *YouTube.* February 2. Accessed December 8, 2021. https://www.youtube.com/watch?v=jjXyqcx-mYY.

n.d. "What Percentage of Businesses Fail in the First Year? (Plus Top Causes of Business Failure)." *FreshBooks.* Accessed November 24, 2021. https://www.freshbooks.com/hub/startup/what-percentage-of-businesses-fail-first-year.

Wikipedia. n.d. "2008 United States presidential election." *Wikipedia.* Accessed December 7, 2021. https://en.wikipedia.org/wiki/2008_United_States_presidential_election.

n.d. "Winfrey, Oprah." *National Women's Hall of Fame.*
Accessed December 7, 2021.
https://www.womenofthehall.org/inductee/oprah-
winfrey/.

World Fantasy Convention. n.d. "Winners." *World
Fantasy Convention.* Accessed December 7,
2021.
http://www.worldfantasy.org/awards/winners/.

World Horror Convention. n.d. "WHC - Grand Master."
World Horror Convention. Accessed December 7,
2021.
http://www.worldhorrorconvention.com/whc2009/G
randMaster.html.

www.ingramcontent.com/pod-product-compliance
Lightning Source LLC
Chambersburg PA
CBHW020434130626
46549CB00001B/141